PEACEFUL ENDINGS
guiding the walk to the end of life
and beyond

The Comfort in their Journey Series
by Trish Laub

A Most Meaningful Life
my dad and Alzheimer's
a guide to living with dementia

Peaceful Endings
guiding the walk to the end of life and beyond
steps to take before and after

Through the Rabbit Hole
navigating the maze of providing care
a quick guide to care options and decisions

PEACEFUL ENDINGS
guiding the walk to the end of life and beyond

steps to take before and after

Trish Laub

PSM Publishing

To purchase:

www.TrishLaub.com 720-288-0772
6845 Osprey Ct Highlands Ranch CO
80130

Dedication

*to all those who have and will allow me
the privilege, trust and honor
of walking them through their final days*

While I am eternally grateful for the time I had with my mom and dad, especially that I nearly lived with them for the last two-plus years of their lives, and while I feel a tinge of "guilt" for having had my mom and dad for so many years, 57 years was simply not enough.

Death changes everything!
Time changes nothing...
I still miss the sound of your voice,
the wisdom in your advice,
the stories of your life and
just being in your presence.
So no, time changes nothing,
I miss you as much today
as I did the day you died.
I just miss you!
Unknown

ACKNOWLEDGEMENTS

with special thanks to both Mom and Dad,

my husband, Chris, who supported my absence during this experience as well as the creation of this project,

my sisters, Barbara and Nancy, who lived my experience with me yet have their own experiences and stories to share,

my daughter Justine, who is my inspiration for all things,

the friends (Janice, Karen, Julia, Mia, Teilene and others) who have carried me through the dark times,

those who have encouraged me to shine a light down the path for those who come next,

Roseanne Geisel (editor), Joanne Wagner (author photographer), Krista Lee (logo and graphic designer), and Sophia Taylor (website/branding) all of whose excellence is unsurpassed,

Deb Sheppard, medium and mentor, who helped me with the "Great Clearing," making this project possible,

all of the caregivers who loved my parents and taught me so much: *Margery, Debbie, Lucia, Ann, Ruth, Shawn, David* and *Angel,* as well as many others who provided not only care but unconditionally gave love; they are all extraordinary people and I am proud to know them and to call them family,

Skye who was a constant source of support and perspective, a wealth of information on the medical field and, last but not least, inspiration,

and especially, Cindy, our Hospice RN/Case Manager, who showed me the path to a peaceful end of life.

and finally a very special thank you to all those who agreed to be what I call my "small book" readers, those who read and provided invaluable feedback on the content: *Justine, Janice, Karen, Skye, Cathe, Margery, Ellen, Judy, Elisabeth, Susie, Klaralee, Debbie and Chris.*

And, thank you to the following for providing commentary on the topics contained in this book:

Katz, Look & Onorato, P.C., and attorney, Klaralee Charlton, who also guided my family through the estate planning and administration processes,

Shine Investment Advisory Services and advisors Judy Shine and Elisabeth Jacobson,

Deborah Neisen, LCSW.

CONTENTS

Chapter 2
UNDERSTANDING ESTATE PLANNING ...

Chapter 6
AFTER TRANSITION ...

Chapter 7
SETTLING AN ESTATE ...

NOTES TO THE READER

Citation of Information

This book presents a conceptual understanding of information, terms, and statistics intended to assist you in a conversation with, and in asking questions of, a professional. Information, unless specifically cited, was provided to me during conversations with professionals or through research of many reliable sources. I have tried to simplify it for non-professionals.

Patient Advocacy

Patient advocacy is **the most important role** in regard to caring for another, and can literally be the difference between life and death. The topic is mentioned in every book of the Comfort in Their Journey book series. It is discussed in Chapters 6 and 11 of *A Most Meaningful Life* and Chapter 1 of *Peaceful Endings*. However, if you only read one chapter in the entire series, please read **The Need for Patient Advocacy... the most important role,** Chapter 2 in *"Through The Rabbit Hole."*

Pronouns

At some point in your life, it is almost certain that you will be responsible for the care of another person. It may be a parent, a sibling, a child or a friend. It may be a loved one, and it may be someone for whom you do not feel love. The gender and age will vary. These variables make it difficult when writing a book and having to reference the person for whom you are responsible for providing care. Therefore, in this text, in regard to the gender, the pronoun "their," as a genderless person, may be used.

About the Ladybugs

The ladybug has been an obsession for me since I was very young and began to collect them. My dad named his fishing boats Ladybug and Ladybug II. The use of the ladybug is an homage to my dad, and the red color, my mom's favorite and her most recent nail color, an homage to her.

Comfort in their Jurney
with *Trish Laub*

You may notice that the *Comfort in Their Journey* logo incorporates the ladybug as the "o" in the word journey.

The open-winged ladybug appears at the top of special sections, such as the Dedication and the start of the Contents, and on the page prior to the start of each chapter.

The closed-winged ladybug appears at the start of each subchapter. In addition, while all information in the book is important, the presence of two closed-winged ladybugs is used to indicate information that requires additional attention. The presence of three closed-winged ladybugs indicates especially critical information.

Knowledge is Power.
Francis Bacon

PREFACE ...

an unlikely expert ...
and "short is the new black"

I became an unlikely "expert"; it's as simple as that. I am not a medical, legal, or financial professional. My expertise is derived from the full-time care of my parents, one with Alzheimer's, for whom I delivered the total care and the end-of-life experience that my parents desired.

In the book "Outliers," the author Malcolm Gladwell speaks to what truly makes someone reach their potential for success. He shares that more than IQ, and in addition to many other factors, practice is key to becoming successful. The principle states that 10,000 hours of "practice" or experience that pushes the skill set to the brink are needed to achieve mastery in any field.

Recently there was an ad for Denver's UCHealth in which Peyton Manning says: "It takes 10,000 hours to become an expert at something. But what happens at 20,000 hours? Or 30,000 hours? What happens when you dedicate yourself to it? Do you become something greater? A leader? A mentor? An innovator? At a certain point, it seems, you stop playing the game and start changing it."

My experience puts me well over 12,000 hours of "practice." Does it make me an expert? Maybe, but only on what I experienced. And after experiencing what I have, it might have seemed "easy" to just walk away and never talk about it or share what I have learned with anyone. To simply "move on." But, I couldn't do it -- walk away with all that I have learned and experienced. It became a "calling," the desire to share in hopes that it might help even one other person thrive in a situation which many times offers only frustration and often defeat. A calling, but was I an expert? Yes, and I am qualified.

What am I qualified to offer? I offer my story and my experience. It is highly likely that during your lifetime you will be responsible for the care of a person with a severe health issue and equally as likely that it will be during the final years and days of that person's life. I offer you the opportunity to *thrive* throughout the process, to think and then take action.

I am here to offer you information, some direction and suggested questions to ask.

- I am not a medical professional; I am not providing medical advice.
- I am not a legal professional; I am not providing legal advice.
- I am not a financial professional; I am not providing financial advice.

During my experience, I needed information I didn't know how to find, and I needed it quickly. Since my experience, I have found that there are hundreds of books and organizations offering pieces of the information I needed. And while the Internet offers information, extreme caution and verification are necessary to ensure accurate and useful advice. In many cases I didn't even know where to look for it or the terminology to Google or to ask. In other cases, I had too little time to find, read and understand it all. I needed the Reader's Digest version of everything. I needed a guide: a clear, concise and useable quick reference. With that in mind, I have adopted the philosophy that "short is the new black" – it is not the volume of words but the value of them that is useful; that providing you with lists and bullet points, things to consider, questions to ask and leads to follow are the most helpful delivery of information.

I also want to state up front that many factors, ranging from geographic proximity to financial resources to flexibility of work schedules, determine what is possible for every family or caregiving team. Each family or caregiving team will handle things in a way suitable for them and the person relying on them. My hope is to provide you tips and spark ideas that work for you.

In short, I became an unlikely expert; I have lived what I have to share.

No one gets out alive.
Trish Laub

PROLOGUE ...

death in America

In America we prepare for the beginning of life, the arrival of a new soul, a baby, with gender reveals, baby showers, excitement and good wishes. Choices for the birthing process include everything from hospitals, facilities and medical doctors to a home water birth with assistance from a midwife. Pain management options include medications and a doula to provide support and comfort prior, during and after the birth. The phrase "birth plan" is often used. We offer our love and time to do whatever is needed to welcome the new baby and help the happy, but tired, new parents.

In stark contrast, we do our best to ignore the fact that every life ends. We are a culture that denies death and therefore its dignity.

Up until the 1940s, most people died at home. Life was hard, and people didn't live as long. Families were centralized and cohesive; women were primarily at home and able to care for family. "Next of kin" was the norm for medical and legal decisions, and because people generally didn't own much property, settlement was not much of an issue. Medical care was both curative and palliative, providing comfort, as there were fewer medicines and limited technology. Death was a more natural and familiar process. Grieving began after the loss.

The situation began to change after World War II. Now families sometimes are separated by great distances, women work outside the home, and two-career households are common. Power of attorney is now necessary for medical decisions, and an executor or trustee must be identified for

1

estate settlement and asset distribution. Life expectancy has increased in large part due to medical advances and technology. Due to better medical management and extended life expectancy, people now often live longer with chronic illness. End of life once took place in the family home and now, more often than not, takes place in a facility. We now grieve throughout the process, as well as after the loss.

Dr. Craig Bowron, in his essay, *Our unrealistic views of death through a doctor's eyes,* expresses the downside of medical advances and resultant treatment. In this piece, published in The Washington Post in 2012, Dr. Bowron raises several serious issues about prolonging life just because we can.

In summary, Dr. Bowron states that we have become a culture that is unfamiliar with the deterioration that comes with age and have rarely witnessed the process of death. No matter how much medicine and technology are available, and even if we can avoid disease, the body wears out and the person dies. We have become a society of many individuals with several chronic conditions held together by medicine. Modern medicine has made death seem more of an option than a natural conclusion. In an attempt to feel that we are doing everything we can for a loved one, we go to medicine for more tests and treatments. But at what cost? It is inhumane to extend life without considering whether more time is worth enduring additional suffering.

> At a certain stage of life,
> aggressive medical treatment
> can become sanctioned torture.
> Craig Bowron, M.D.

People hope that their loved ones will die naturally, and they envision them passing away peacefully in their sleep. Almost everyone dies of illness, and the process requires planning if it is to be peaceful. Pre-emptive preparedness, specifying what you want to happen in the event that your time is approaching, is the best gift you can give to your loved ones. It eliminates the stress and conflict that arises from having to decide whether or not to treat an illness, and then sometimes choosing treatment that may cause harm and discomfort with no real benefit.

With a little thought and a roadmap, we ensure ourselves, and those we love, of aging and ultimately dying with dignity. But we must spend time planning while we are well, or it is unlikely that we will achieve the end of life that we want. According to information on a Stanford School of Medicine website, studies show that close to 80% of people want to die in their home, yet today only approximately 20% do. Planning is required to ensure your wishes.

The problem our culture faces is not a medical one, but rather a human one. We deny that death is a natural conclusion to life, and we neither acknowledge nor plan for it. It is our nature to prolong life, made possible with dependence on medicine and technology, and to feel that we are doing everything possible to fight death. But often, in a misguided attempt to increase longevity, we compromise quality. So what can we do to truly help our loved ones? We can be there for them and tend to their body and spirit. We can give them our time and our love. And we can let them go, with the most dignified death possible.

What if we put the same energy and love into the ending of life, the ushering out of a soul, that we do into welcoming a soul? What if we embraced the process that results in a soul transitioning out of this life as we do birth? What if our goal was to ensure death its dignity?

All life topics are heavy...
every single phase of life
is inclusive of the same elements:
having a baby, raising or being a child,
adolescence, young adulthood,
middle adulthood, aging
and then dying.
They each have such ease
and such chaos.
The writer's responsibility is
to invite the reader into the topic
and lessen any fears with information.
Skye O'Neil PA-C, Blue Heron LLC

INTRODUCTION ...

I am here to talk about death

Just 48 hours after moving across the country to Colorado, where my parents lived, I found myself at the beginning of a 2 ½ year caregiving odyssey. My two sisters and I had to rapidly assume responsibility for all of the medical, insurance, legal and financial aspects of my parents' lives. Even the first step of understanding their estate planning was overwhelming. I had entered a world that used a language entirely new to me. I had to learn new terms and their definitions in order to ask intelligent questions.

Sometime later, my husband's son lost his father-in-law with no notice. He had no last will and testament, owned assets and his affairs were neither documented nor in order. While the family struggled with the loss, they were also lost as to what their loved one had wanted for the end of his life. Even after death, my stepson said, "No one wants to talk about it."

Well, I am here to talk about it! I am here to talk about all of it, from the initial realization that the end of life is inevitable for all of us, through one's experience during their final days on Earth. If you are the caregiver for one of the most important people in your life, it is emotionally and sometimes physically exhausting. But you will never regret the opportunity to show your love during this time. And whether the person has an end of life plan or does not, let the caregiving role remind you to make things as easy as possible for your loved ones when you need care. An end of life plan and a financial plan create a clear roadmap for those who will be left to execute your final wishes and to settle your estate.

I wish that I had had a guide to help me understand the lexicon and the process of end of life, to illuminate the unknown and allay my fears, and to allow me to thrive throughout the process. This is that guide.

🐞🐞 For the sake of ease, please note that I use the terms death/dying (the event) and transition/transitioning (the process of dying) interchangeably.

Some are lost in the fire,
others are built from it.
Adapted from Betty Rocker

Chapter 1

CRISIS MANAGEMENT ...

finding stable ground

A crisis is a single moment in which life changes forever, like a spark that ignites a potentially all-consuming fire. Some people see it coming, but most do not. Some have already eased on, and found a rhythm, to the caregiving path and others have no notice or prior experience with care. Some think that they are well prepared, others know that they are not, but most find that they become engulfed in the "flames", threatened by consumption.

Crises come in many forms. My parents had each lived nearly 90 years without any real major medical crises. Dad had Alzheimer's, and while my parents needed some assistance, there had been no life-changing crisis—until there was. That was when we needed crisis management. Six months later while still containing the "flames" from Dad's crisis, Mom had a medical crisis that escalated us into a five-alarm situation.

In addition to my experience with my parents, I have witnessed other forms of crisis. My dear friend Jan sprinted through her husband's first bout with cancer to the finish line, a cure, without crisis. Round two, a second cancer, resulted in a crisis which nearly consumed her and jettisoned her into a marathon of care and treatment. My mother-in-law was diagnosed with a prognosis of a couple of months, plunging the family into crisis. Only five weeks later, she was in the hospital and put on hospice. Ten days later she peacefully passed away in her home surrounded by love. It

11

had been six weeks from diagnosis, barely time for the family to even comprehend what had happened.

We cannot always prevent the crisis, but we can prevent the crisis from consuming us. Everyone responds differently. Some people retreat from the heat of the fire and stay away. Others stand in the center of the fire and are consumed by it. The best that anyone can do is to manage the crisis instead of letting it manage them, to become the fire and use its clarity and single purpose to be fueled by it.

Your first task may well be crisis management. The reason this is so important is that the other person needs you at your best to oversee their care and the path through their final days.

The Crisis May Be More Than Just the Diagnosis
A loved one may recently have been diagnosed with a condition that is treatable but incurable, or even terminal. Caregiving has become an urgent need. A variety of emotions arise in these situations. At the very least, it is overwhelming. No matter how prepared you are for a loved one's death, no matter how much you want what is best for another, you are never truly ready.

> I've come to realize that nothing in life
> prepares us for losing someone we love,
> nothing.
> Angels at My Door

Often what happens is that the realization of another's impending death is a trigger for many other things: confronting your mortality, reviewing one's own life, fear of being alone, fear of merely surviving instead of thriving during the crisis, and fear of life beyond their death. It can be compounded, as being faced with a loss can bring back the experience and emotion of every previous loss. Each new loss can feel cumulative. When the situation involves an ill parent, some people feel a "connected loss," because the surviving parent may feel the effects of caregiving and be grieving.

No matter how prepared you are, there are emotional stages that may be experienced. Elisabeth Kubler-Ross identified the stages experienced by terminally ill patients after diagnosis and found them to be experienced by loved ones after the diagnosis and beyond death. The stages of shock and denial, anger, bargaining, depression, and acceptance may be experienced in any order and may be experienced multiple times. The truth is that, as a patient or a caregiver, when you hear that an illness is not curable, no matter how strong you are or how accepting you are of the diagnosis, it is normal to start the grieving process. Everyone is allowed some time to simply settle into the new reality. But then you either get up and move on to caring for the other person or seek professional help with the crisis.

> Sometimes we have to be broken down
> so that we can be rebuilt
> into what we're actually meant to be.
> Unknown

Understanding What You Are Facing
My friend Jan's experience with her husband's first diagnosis with lung cancer was a full on sprint, from a painstakingly

slow, atypical and inconclusive diagnosis through successful surgery and other treatments.

She was the perfect athlete, on top of her game, stride after stride, each beautiful and strong. Jan learned all the skills necessary to quarterback the team responsible for her husband's care, in chase of a cure. Eventually, her husband was pronounced "cured;" it seemed the race had been won. One month later, her husband was diagnosed with the same type of cancer in his left lung. Overwhelmed by the ramifications of a second diagnosis and spiraling into crisis, Jan simply hit the wall, or quite literally the floor and then the bed. Panic had set in, and this formidable woman had gone into full-blown tilt, losing her normally solid bearings. After four days in bed, sick with the flu and unable to stop crying, she asked for help. She needed help grasping their new reality and developing her perspective on it. Once she did, she became stable again and could move forward and provide the care that her husband needed.

   ☼☼ Before going further, I want to pause here to emphasize that caregivers must monitor themselves to ensure that they stay well. This is not a selfish act, but something that will benefit the person for whom you are caring. If you feel that the toll is great, in addition to talking to another loved one or friend, please see your doctor and or a therapist.

Once Jan was on her feet again, I explained that the first bout of cancer was a sprint, but this time it would be a marathon, one for which she had no training. She had been beating herself up, criticizing herself for no longer being strong. She was exhausted from her recently completed sprint and the prospect of the upcoming marathon. There was nothing wrong with her. She was just tired.

She had hit the wall, crushed by the overwhelming reality, responsibility, fear of the unknown and fear of the future. We talked about what needed to happen for her to thrive. In Jan's case, she needed someone to help her get back on her feet again by providing support and perspective, and possibly a professional to provide additional perspective and appropriate treatment.

Understanding what you are facing -- whether your crisis is a sprint or a marathon -- and facing it rested, is critical to your success at managing the crisis.

Facing Reality and Your Fears
When Jan was faced with her husband's second diagnosis, she said that her mind "was filled with hundreds of thoughts and would not calm down." She told me what was on her mind, and all of her fears were rational. She feared losing her husband and best friend, being alone during and after, and living life by herself. It had triggered her realization of her own mortality, her stage in life, and a review of that life, as well as other life and death issues.

You gain strength, courage, and confidence
by every experience in which you really
stop to look fear in the face.
You must do the thing
which you think you cannot do.
Eleanor Roosevelt

After identifying her fears, she consulted me about what could be done to allay them, as she realized that they were not useful in the process of helping her husband. Jan understood that anxiety and panic are not useful and that a plan is. We spent time:

- Identifying information and documents that should be gathered and placed in a file
- Developing a budget for them, to provide peace of mind for Jan and to identify their financial ability to provide care for her husband
- Discussing the information that would be necessary when her husband was in his final days and afterward, including hospice organizations and cremation and ceremony arrangements, and who could help
- Talking about the fact that the future journey was likely going to be a roller coaster, and that she therefore needed a game plan to stay stable

> Everybody needs a person who just knows...
> so you don't have to say it.
> Jan, my friend and wife of cancer patient

Jan was a very accomplished, capable and smart woman and yet she felt none of that when faced with her current crisis. To address her fear of being alone after her husband passed, she needed a little more perspective. We reviewed her past as a single woman who bought her own townhouse, owned a car, managed a major business and ran a business out of her home. And we identified her circle of friends who were genuinely willing to do whatever she needed. She had no need to worry.

Once she had identified her fears, she needed to identify those who could help with them. Of course, she had me to help with the process. When caring for my parents, my family reached out to various professionals for assistance with allaying my parents' fears: my parent's lawyer, financial advisor, insurance providers and accountant.

F.E.A.R has two meanings:
Forget **E**verything **A**nd **R**un
Face **E**verything **A**nd **R**ise
The choice is yours.
Unknown

In the end Jan said, "It all boils down to fear."

Perspective
Perspective is a particular attitude toward or way of seeing something. Shifting one's perspective is the key to easing the burden of a diagnosis and the resultant crisis.

Accept – then act.
Whatever the present moment contains,
accept it as if you had chosen it.
Always work with it, not against it.
This will miraculously transform your whole life
Eckhart Tolle

The Rollercoaster Ride
Some of us, as children, appreciated and even looked forward to a rollercoaster ride. The thrill of the easy chug up toward the sky, followed by the long sharp drop that left your stomach at the top, and the straightaway surge around a tight corner were all causes for squeals and screams somewhere between terror and delight. The bigger the rollercoaster, the better. As we age, somehow the thrill is not the same, is not appreciated, is not even wanted.

The first step toward thriving during the crisis is to know that there will be ups and downs. It is important to know that experiencing various emotions during caregiving is healthy and valuable: laugh, cry, feel joy and sorrow. The difference is that you should be able to reset your emotional responses in a reasonable amount of time. So, if you are stuck in a crying jag for days or the emotional roller coaster is making you too anxious to function, then you should talk to a professional about coping strategies. Part of being able to handle the highs and the lows is understanding that they will come, sometimes without notice, and also knowing that you can ride through them.

> You never know how strong you are
> until being strong is the only choice you have.
> Bob Marley

After the initial crisis, finding stability and your footing may provide you with a surge of energy and positivity. You may feel strong, invincible and almost high. Enjoy it, for it will not last. Know that there will be good days and there will be less good days. Learn to ride through them with the knowledge that either kind of day will not last. Use all the resources and tools available to you to bring yourself up when you are down. Utilize your tribe and anything else that helps to pick you up. (See *Self-Care is a Four Letter Word; It Is Self ... LOVE!* below.) Be easy with yourself for you are still strong, merely weary. When you are down, don't fight it; ride through it and the rollercoaster will again rise for another round. When you are up, savor it. There may come a rhythm to the ups and downs, and they may become less drastic. The better you get at acknowledging them and not reacting to them, the less control they will have over you.

You Are Not the Patient

In a crisis, it is easy to be consumed by the diagnosis and to even let the diagnosis become a part of you, as though it is yours. It is important to keep the diagnosis separate from you. It is not yours. You do not have the illness. They do. Unless there have been two identical diagnoses, one for you and one for the other, "we" don't have it, such as "we" don't have cancer.

To be clear, something is certainly happening to you, but it is quite a different experience. Your experience is primarily, at least initially, emotional and mental. It may become physical later if you do not care for yourself. Their experience is initially primarily physical or mental. Depending on the path of the illness, their experience may become emotional. In all cases, the one diagnosed is the expert on their diagnosis.

There were many times when my parents would defer to me to answer a professional's question, but I never answered without their deference. Because of the seriousness of an illness, there were many times when a professional would enter the room and ask what I had decided about my parents' treatment. I always said clearly that I was not the patient, and that it was my parents' decision, not mine. I would then explain that I merely gathered information to present to my parents; they were in control and would make their own decisions. If they were unable to make a decision for any reason, I would state the decision that my family felt was best and then ask for my parents' concurrence, by saying "is that okay with you?" Even if they were unable to respond, I had asked.

19

The Diagnosis Should Not Be All Consuming.
Again, perspective is the key to managing your crisis. It was helpful when I pointed out to Jan that her husband could pass away from something other than cancer, and that in fact, she could pass away first. The intention was not to diminish the severity of her husband's diagnosis but rather to illustrate that while cancer is a life-limiting concern, it should not be an all-consuming focus.

In another context, a myopic focus based only on a specific existing illness can result in a missed diagnosis of other issues. For example, as I've said, my mom had stage 4 metastatic colon cancer. She developed a large tumor in her abdomen, which was assumed to be part of the colon cancer. However, it was something totally separate and required different treatment. A myopic focus would have prevented us from realizing it was unrelated to her colon cancer, and would have resulted in improper treatment, allowing the tumor to grow to crush her organs, causing tremendous suffering.

What is Your Belief System?
By belief system, I am not necessarily or exclusively referring to religious or spiritual beliefs, although they may well be a part of your belief system. Your belief system includes your values, morals, ethics; and thoughts on your life and the lives of others; and on death and the existence of souls. Clarity on your belief system is helpful. It allows you to find perspective on what is happening and what it means to you.

Your belief system is what allows you to survive the crisis by making another's wellbeing and quality of life a priority. None of us want to lose someone, and all losses are different. We know that we might lose a spouse or friend, we even expect that we will lose our parents, but it is unimaginable to think of losing a child. But the reality is the same, we don't want them to stay on earth with us if it means that they are sick or in pain. In actuality, their ultimate wellbeing and quality of life are the priority. It is in their best interest that we selflessly let them go, as opposed to selfishly wanting them not to go, providing the best possible ending.

Accepting Your New Normal

Each day of our lives is different. No one knows how it will be different, but it will not be the same as the day before. Some days even start with a clear plan and end up far from what we had anticipated. The new crisis is only one of many reasons why your day, and life, will be different.

It is easy to wonder when your life will return to what it was prior to the crisis. It never will. Your life will now find a new normal, just as it does every day when you encounter change. It's as simple, and as complicated, as that. As always, you have a choice to fight the change with fear, stress and possibly disappointment, or to accept the change and your new normal.

Part of your new normal is the awareness, especially as end of life approaches, that you never really know what the last words you will speak to your loved one will be. Words have power: the power to heal, the power to hurt, the power to cause regret for a remaining lifetime. Be mindful, as you should be every day but especially when end of life is approaching, that it is even more important to remember that what you are saying might be the last thing you say to the person. Ask yourself if that is what you really want. Crisis is stressful and frustration and fatigue can come out as angry words that we don't even mean. We are all human. If you say something you regret, go back and own it, make no excuse for it but instead correct it, and forgive yourself. Even if that person is unconscious, say it out loud to them as they will hear you.

Self-Care is a Four-Letter Word; It Is Self ... LOVE!

Rest and self-care are so important.
When you take the time to replenish your spirit,
it allows you to serve others from the overflow.
You cannot serve from an empty vessel.
Eleanor Brownn, Self-Care Coach

Caring for yourself is often compared with being asked by flight attendants to place your oxygen mask over your mouth before helping your child with their mask. If you do not take care of yourself, you cannot help those who need your help. In times of crisis, it is easy to feel and believe that you do not have time to take care of yourself. Make this a priority! It is the difference in the quality of care you can provide and the decisions you will make.

Sometimes doing something for yourself, for as little as a few minutes, is all that is needed to sustain your well-being. I teach a dance movement class, but while caring for my parents, my schedule only allowed me to be a substitute teacher. I am so happy that I did not give it up altogether. Whenever I really needed a break, especially one I did not feel I could take, I would get a call to teach for a colleague. The class I teach requires my full attention and an awareness of how my body is feeling. I was not able to teach and remain in the world of providing care at the same time. For one hour, I was in a different place, one in which I could thrive with no decisions required of me. After that hour I was rejuvenated and fresh, ready to face whatever my journey held for me.

> A good laugh and a long sleep
> are the two best cures for anything.
> Irish Proverb

Your respite might be a cup of coffee, a yoga class, a massage, a nap, a conversation with a trusted friend or simply sitting in silence. Whatever your source of rejuvenation, find it and do it, for yourself and for the sake of others. Make it a priority.

Information, Friend or Foe?
We live in the Information Age, the age of computers, the internet. digital communication, and social media where much of the information in delivered in sound bites via technology. We now have access to more information than we could imagine let alone comprehend even a decade ago. Access to all of this information is a double-edged sword offering the possibility of usefulness with the risk of harmful unreliability, inaccuracy, or misinformation. Computers crunch data as fast as it can be gathered, revealing information in the form of patterns and statistical probabilities. But keep the information generated in perspective, as there will always be outliers. With all information proceed with caution, consider the source, the accuracy and the relevance, and evaluate its usefulness. Information has the power to either feed or ease the crisis.

Prognosis, is it useful?
A prognosis is a medical provider's opinion or forecast of the probable course and outcome of a diagnosis, particularly

regarding the chances of recovery. While based on medical evidence, there are always outliers. In some situations, and for some people, knowing the worst-case prognosis is helpful in planning remaining quality time and care needs. In other cases, knowing a prognosis may only lead to obsession and assumption, sometimes starting a mental countdown, which is not constructive. The question to be asked in regard to deciding if you want to know a prognosis is "will the information be useful to me in a positive way?"

Whether or not knowing a prognosis will be helpful or hurtful is a personal decision. My mom had been diagnosed with stage 4 metastatic colon cancer that was in her liver. I did **not** want a prognosis. I knew that it was in all likelihood terminal, but I did not want to buy into an end time. My mom was strong and determined, and I knew that if anyone could beat the odds, she could. After her passing, I was told what the original prognosis was and it fit her timeline, even though in my mind, she ultimately passed away from something other than her terminal diagnosis. My mother-in-law was officially diagnosed with lung cancer a week before my husband's and my departure date for a very special trip. Because of the nature of the trip, we had purchased trip insurance and were willing to cancel the trip. In this situation, a private conversation with her oncologist and a requested prognosis were very helpful in determining how much time we might have with her and what we should do about our trip. Although I was told by a medical professional that medical providers tend to overestimate the patient's life expectancy by as much as 50%, in the end, the prognosis for both my mom and my mother-in-law were nearly exact. In the end, knowing the prognosis would not have been useful in one situation, but was in the other.

Sharing Information

You will have to decide whether or not you will share information about your crisis, and if so, what and how much you will share. Sharing information can be energizing or depleting, depending on a combination of the reaction of those who will receive the information and their expectation to be kept updated.

The decision starts with whether or not the person living with the illness wants the diagnosis shared and with whom. Many other factors must be considered in the decision to share a diagnosis or not. Every diagnosis is different and the decision to share it will depend on whether or not you feel it is helpful to the person with the illness.

If you have chosen to share the diagnosis, your next decision is to determine if, how and with whom you will provide updates. Done with forethought, sharing updates can be a great source of support. Otherwise sharing updates can become an exhausting, depleting and unnecessary responsibility. Sometimes one in your "tribe" can take on the responsibility of disseminating updates you have approved.

There are several options for sharing information: phone calls, which are time consuming but which may be appropriate for some information and some receivers; text threads, several of which can be created for different groups of supporters; and sending emails using distributions lists similar to the concept of using different text threads. Caringbridge.com is a website that allows the creation, free of charge, of a personal health journal in which entries can be posted to document the patient's journey. It helps maintain energetic boundaries by allowing family and friends to have access to information and updates without requiring the investment of time and energy to speak with each person who cares. Those who choose to follow the journey can post messages of support to each journal entry. Caringbridge allows privacy settings so that a health journal can be made public to and searchable by all Caringbridge registrants, or private and accessible only to those you invite.

Second Guessing is Not Useful
Especially early on in a crisis, caregivers may have the contradictory feelings that they have a huge amount of information to absorb and that information is insufficient to make necessary decisions. I live by the belief that there are no bad decisions as long as you make the best decision you can at the time with the information you have. If you do that, you can be at peace that you made the best decision possible. That belief has saved me the anguish of second guessing or playing the "what if" game. No good comes from that game, and your energy is better spent offering your best caregiving. I also knew that in some cases if I made a decision and later received better information, I could change my previous decision.

The Internet: Not All Information is Good
The internet is a vast source of information, the quality of which is variable; this is particularly true for medical websites. If you search the web be sure that the website you access is reputable. For example, NIH.gov is a reputable source of information which includes medical information and a dictionary. NCBI.NLM.NIH.gov is a resource for medical studies. For me, other websites, such as WebMD provide a good place to start for basic information and to help identify questions to ask your doctors. In addition, keep in mind that very rare extremes have happened to someone, somewhere and it will be documented on the internet. A good percentage of what you read on the internet will not be your experience. Incorrect information can cause unneeded

pain and fear. Keep information in perspective and use caution.

False Evidence Appearing Real = F.E.A.R.

Finding Your Footing

Once you have managed the crisis and feel stable, you need to begin putting one foot in front of the other. Start by gathering the information you need; begin to document absolutely everything, whether it's a call to a physician or a dose of medication administered, because you can't expect yourself to remember everything under stressful circumstances; create a plan; identity your care team; and finally deal with incorporating family into the process.

Gather Information

The first thing you need to do is to gather some very important information listed below.

- Power of attorneys - medical and durable
- Advance directive, DNR (Do not resuscitate order), end-of-life decisions
- Identification and insurance cards
- The Emergency Book (see *Through the Rabbit Hole* for detail)
- Medical records

After you have taken a quick breath you may need to know the location of and/or to find the following items.

- Important papers such as: wills, trusts, birth certificate, government-issued id, marriage license
- Health, life, and long-term care insurance policies
- Banking information
- Investment information

- Deeds and titles
- Safe deposit box information and "hidden" valuables

Document Everything
From the first diagnosis through the end of the health crisis, *document everything.* With every medical crisis there is an overwhelming amount of information and paperwork. Although you may have clearly heard and understood a provider's explanation, it is more often than not impossible to remember exactly what was said after returning home. The solution is easy. Immediately purchase several spiral notebooks and a couple of three-ring binders. They will become invaluable to you. I recommend that you start with one spiral notebook that will be like a diary of the journey, and use a new spiral notebook for each event such as a hospitalization. As you receive documents, begin to put them in the three-ring binders. You will likely create a notebook for medical documents, insurance claims, appointments, medication, etc.

Create a Plan
Now that you have gathered the necessary information, you are ready to create a plan.

> A goal without a plan is just a wish.
> Antoine de Saint-Exupery

Creating a plan starts with defining your philosophy and goals, and developing a strategy. From there you can create a care plan with specific actions. If your situation requires the provision of care for the person diagnosed, see *Through the Rabbit Hole*, which provides a quick guide to care options and decisions. Your plan should be based on the values and wishes of the person for whom you will be providing care. An understanding of estate planning will be needed

(Chapter 2, *A Most Meaningful Life* and *Through the Rabbit Hole* are helpful resources for the process of creating a plan.)

Identify Your Care Team
Your care team consists of everyone responsible for the care of the patient. For healthcare, this may include a primary care physician, specialists including palliative and hospice care providers, therapists, and caregivers when needed. There are other types of "care," tasks that involve legal, financial, insurance and household issues to name a few. Professionals, family members, and anyone else providing any type of care are part of the team.

The most important person on the team is the one managing the care team. They are the person, possibly a power of attorney or a family member, who is responsible for overseeing and coordinating the entire process. They are what I call the team bus driver, providing direction and ensuring that everyone arrives at the same destination. Without this person, no one is driving the bus, and without coordination or direction, everyone is operating separately, possibly duplicating effort or even heading to different destinations.

Patient Advocacy
Even in the final stage of life, the patient needs an advocate. This is a very specific job on the care team. A patient advocate becomes the "quarterback" of the healthcare team, acting as keeper of the healthcare information, coordinator of the healthcare plan, and representative for the best interests of the patient. The patient advocate should be someone the patient trusts, who has good communication skills, is comfortable speaking with healthcare providers and is available to attend appointments if needed. They become a spokesperson for the patient, and sometimes for the family,

and the center of information and communication in regard to the patient's healthcare.

For end-of-life care this means ensuring that the patient's wishes are carried out and that their needs during the transition process are met. While death may be imminent, it is important to protect the patient's end-of-life process so that it occurs on the patient's terms, not as a result of a care plan oversight or medical error. This is a critical topic that is discussed in *A Most Meaningful Life* and detailed in *Through the Rabbit Hole*.

Family and the Crisis
The family's role is to provide comfort, protection, patient advocacy, respect, dignity and love. Family may or may not entirely consist of blood relatives.

Briefly, my experience is that crisis brings out all dormant family dynamics and issues. Unhealed wounds resurface. While the patient is the focus, it is not about just them. It is also about the close circle of family and extended "family" (possibly including any caregivers) who are affected by the process. How the group functions during the crisis and throughout the process of the end of life will determine the future relationships of the group members. In the long run, it is an opportunity for you to rise above or even change your past patterns. Others may continue their past negative behavior patterns but you have choice to respond differently. It is a growth opportunity to focus on the objective, the patient, and not fall prey to unconstructive interactions. This is not intended to sound negative but the stress of crisis, as well as the end of life, creates an environment in which people often do not function at their best. All you can do is to be aware and to make the best choices for your own behavior, as well as your responses to the behaviors of others.

ᚖ ᚖ ᚖ Unless an interaction with family members, or friends, is beneficial to the patient, *let it go*. Now is not the time to address negative behaviors or past issues. The only thing that matters is the well-being of the patient and that their needs are being met. Discord is always distressing to the patient.

Some family members live close by and are at the center of the crisis and care, while others live far away and may be more removed. Even among family members who live close, each will participate at different levels of interest, willingness, ability and commitment. Regardless of proximity, and responsibilities and constraints such as children and jobs, every person has the opportunity to contribute positively to the situation. Every person has an ability that can be used, a task that they can do to contribute to the process. Identifying those abilities and tasks and using each person's strengths will access the greatest number of helpers. It is important for each person involved in the care of the patient to communicate their abilities, expectations and needs in a direct, specific, and non-punishing manner. Even those who feel that they cannot contribute should be heard. When family members cannot actively participate, their role is to provide support to those who can. Each person will make their own decision as to if and how they will contribute, and each is to be respected for their decision.

Each person who cares about the patient will go through their own version of what you experienced when the crisis first hit you. Be patient with them and allow them time and space to process, just as you did.

The topic of family is very complex and is more fully detailed in *Through the Rabbit Hole*.

You Are Not Alone

It is helpful to acknowledge your tribe, those who will make the journey through your crisis with you. It is those family members and friends who you can call in the middle of the night and who will talk you through the night or arrive at your door as soon as possible, no questions asked. They are your inner circle of support and deserve updates as often as you are able. Sometimes one in your tribe can take on the responsibility, relieving you of the job, for disseminating updates you have approved.

Your tribe is there, with their varied skill sets, waiting and able to help you at a moment's notice. When you feel most that you are barely holding on, it is your tribe who will hold you up. Let them.

For those who do not have family or friends who can help, there are many organizations waiting to provide assistance. Many churches provide a variety of services, from loaning assistive devices to providing meals and volunteer companions.

👀👀 Every county in the United States is required by federal law to provide information about and assist with access to senior services. These vary and may include case management including comprehensive needs assessment and care plan development, assistance with locating appropriate care, the loaning of assistive devices, transportation options and more. Some counties provide services for multiple counties and share resources. (Google: "find local Area Agency on Aging (followed by the zipcode or county and state)" or visit http://www.n4a.org. Otherwise, call your county and ask to be directed to the senior services department.)

33

Lexicon:
the vocabulary of
a particular language, field, or group.
dictionary.com

Chapter 2

UNDERSTANDING ESTATE PLANNING ...
a new lexicon

As I said in the introduction, after assuming caregiving and medical management responsibilities for our parents, my sisters and I soon began to oversee all other aspects of their lives, including legal and financial. We were overwhelmed and a bit lost. We had each created our own estate plans but needed assistance in understanding the nuances of our parents' plan, as well as their wishes about end of life. We initially struggled with our misconceptions about the role of various representatives. During estate settlement we found that we did not have a clear understanding of the legal and financial components of the estate plan, and we had much to clarify and to learn. While our parents' estate plan was fairly up to date, it needed modification during a time of crisis to ensure that their final wishes were accurately executed. In the end, after completing the settlement of our parents' estate, and inspired by the importance of providing a clear estate plan for those who might care for us one day, we each did a thorough review and update of our individual estate plans.

If you have found yourself, as we did, responsible for understanding the estate plan of another, and even if you have created a plan for yourself, you may be faced with learning a new lexicon, the language specific to the legal world. A knowledge of this terminology is necessary for understanding the estate plan and executing the settlement of another's estate.

The terminology used regarding estate planning, both legal and financial, varies by state but can be defined in general as follows. This terminology is universally understood even if a particular state uses a slightly different term for a concept.

🐞🐞The following is a conceptual understanding of the terms intended to assist you in a conversation with, and in asking questions of, a professional. Please note that the definitions have been written based on conversations I had regarding estate planning and settlement, in regard to myself and my parents, as well as information from many legal sources. I have tried to simplify them for non-lawyers.

🐞🐞🐞 For those who have not done their own estate planning, refer to the Afterword on what to have prepared to help your loved ones care for you and execute your final wishes. It is a great gift you can provide for them, relieving them of having to make decisions without knowing your wishes.

What is Estate Planning?

Estate planning is the process of arranging for the management, administration and distribution of your estate, both during your life and after death. It is most effective when coordinated with financial planning, which allows for maximizing the value of the estate by minimizing income, gift and estate taxes. Estate planning can include planning for incapacity, providing for long term care and instructions for the end-of-life process. Thorough estate planning requires several legal documents which identify various representatives described below.

Estate planning reduces or eliminates uncertainties over the administration of the estate after death. A part of the process of estate settlement is known as **probate**. <u>*There is a misconception that probate is a lengthy and unwanted process, one to be avoided.*</u> This may be true when no estate planning has been legally documented and decisions regarding the distribution of assets must be made by the probate court. When estate planning has been legally documented through a will, upon death the executor must file with probate court for the authority to begin settlement. This is a simple and quick process. If estate planning has been established through the creation of a trust, the successor trustee does **not** have to file with probate court. However, a will is still recommended in addition to a trust, as a catch-all for items not covered by the trust.

Types of Representatives

Individuals who hold the power of attorney, guardians and conservators assist a person **during the life** <u>of the person they represent.</u>

Power of Attorney

A power of attorney is held by someone, not necessarily an attorney, who acts in the best interest of the person while they are **alive**. Power of attorney responsibilities **commence** <u>when the person they represent is unable to do specific tasks for themself or per the terms of the document, and</u> **terminate** <u>upon their death.</u>

For estate planning purposes, there are two types of power of attorney:

1. ***Durable power of attorney*** who has the right to make decisions concerning the person's property (physical and financial) and
2. ***Durable power of attorney for health care decisions***

Guardianship and Conservatorship

A person who is unable to make fully informed personal or financial decisions may need a guardian or conservator if the person has not designated a power of attorney. A guardian or conservator also is necessary if the power of attorney does not want the full responsibility or the decisions of the power of attorney are in question.

A *guardian* assists with a person's <u>housing, medical care and other necessities of life.</u>

A *conservator* assists with a person's <u>financial affairs and is given nearly 100% financial control.</u>

The division in definition allows a person to live and remain personally independent while obtaining assistance with financial issues only. It is common, however, for both services to be appointed for a person.

In some states, there are other terms for these designations. For example, a conservator may be called a guardian of the estate and a guardian may be called a conservator of the person. The important thing to know is the definition of their duties.

The processes for appointment of guardians and conservators are very similar. Both are appointed by a court in procedures that begin with the filing of a petition by the person seeking the appointment, which is often a family member or a power of attorney who is unable to fulfill their duties. There are several steps taken by the court, which may vary from state to state, to determine the need for the request. Once an appointment has been made, the duties of the appointee begin. The appointee is required to report back to the court and is under court supervision. There are procedures for replacing and terminating the appointee's services. Termination requires proof of cause.

Services are offered by specialized businesses as well as many law offices, both of which will assist with the appointment process.

Executor/Executrix/Personal Representative

👀 👀 Executor responsibilities are **effective upon approval by probate court after the death of the person** they are to represent.

An executor is someone who is nominated in the documents associated with a will and serves to oversee the settlement and distribution of assets **not** contained in a trust, *which are items still in the decedent's name.* An executor is sometimes called an executrix, if female, or a personal representative in other states. Executor responsibilities **commence upon approval by probate court after the death of the person they are to represent** and **terminate** when the estate has been settled.

👀 👀 👀 A will *nominates* an executor. An executor has no authority until they have gone through *probate* (a legal process) by submitting an application including the will to probate court (in the county court where the deceased resided). A probate court decides the legal validity of the decedent's will and grants approval, also known as granting probate, therefore officially appointing the executor. A document called *letters testamentary* is then provided. The letters testamentary may need to be presented as proof of authority to act as the executor and to distribute the decedent's assets in the manner specified in the decedent's will.

🐞🐞🐞 If there is no will, a person willing to serve as executor must submit an application to probate court requesting approval to act as executor according to state statutes. In this situation, a document called *letters of administration* is provided.

There are different forms of the probate process: *informal probate* (the heirs/beneficiaries are getting along), *unsupervised formal probate* (there is no reason to anticipate disagreements) and *supervised formal probate* (determined necessary by the court).

Trustee
A trustee is someone designated in the terms of a trust to oversee the management, settlement and distribution of the assets in the trust (see Trusts below). Successor trustee responsibilities **commence** with the incapacitation, resignation or death of the current trustee and **terminate** when:
1. the trust has been dissolved or
2. the trustee resigns their responsibilities, and either a successor trustee or another trustee is designated

Estate Planning Documents
Because probate is a legal process that involves time and effort, it is often desirable to try to avoid it in the estate

settlement process. The method by which the distribution of an asset is specified will determine whether probate is necessary. Any combination of these strategies can be used, and there may be other options available. **A living trust, tenancy, and beneficiary designations supersede, take precedence over, a Last Will and Testament.**

Last Will and Testament

Assets for which a Last Will and Testament (commonly referred to as a will) specifies distribution are distributed by the executor identified in the will and are therefore subject to probate. Because the will must be filed with the county (of the decedent's residence) court, distribution of the assets is on public record. There are three options for distributing assets from a will. First, the assets can be designated to be distributed in their entirety and outright without any restrictions. The second option is to distribute the assets under the specifications of a trust to be created by the will (see Trusts below). Finally, a combination of both can be used with part of the assets distributed outright and part through a trust.

A will is a legal declaration by which a person names one or more persons to manage his or her estate (executor) and provides for the distribution of his or her property at death. This covers property that is **not in a living trust** (see below, including the five benefits a living trust can provide) or other probate-avoidance device (see below).

🐞🐞🐞 A will is the basis of estate planning. *Even when a living trust exists, a will is essential for several reasons.* First a will identifies the distribution for all property not identified as part of a living trust. It can serve as a sort of catch-all, back-up plan for instances when a trust has not been fully

41

funded (see Trusts below) or assets have not yet been transferred. A will can designate that everything not in trust is to be transferred into the trust upon death. *Without a will, any property **not** in a living trust or other probate-avoidance device, such as tenancy or beneficiary designation (see below), will be distributed to your closest relatives in an order determined by state law.* This order may be undesirable. To find your state law, Google: "laws of intestate succession in" followed by your state name.

The property, designated by a will or as part of a living trust, can be distributed **per stirpes**. This distribution approach means that if a beneficiary is deceased, the inherited assets are to filter down to the beneficiary's descendants. Per stirpes also indicates that assets are to be distributed to each branch of a family in equal shares. This can result in members of the same generation receiving different dollar amounts of an asset. **Per capita** distributes the assets equally to a specified group or to the living members of the generation closest to the deceased, with no consideration to further generations.

To provide an example of the difference between per stirpes and per capita, let's say that a person wants to distribute a sum of money among three children, two of which have produced two grandchildren and one of which has produced one grandchild. In the case of a *per capita* distribution, each of the children would receive an equal share. In this example, if all the children were living, each of the three children would receive 1/3rd of the distribution. If any of them had deceased, the amount would be divided by the number of living children. Everyone gets an equal share. No grandchildren would receive any assets.

In the case of a *per stirpes* distribution, the distribution is made to the living relatives at the top of each descendant bloodline. In this example, if all three children were alive, each would receive 1/3rd of the distribution. If any of the children were deceased, their 1/3rd would be split equally between their direct descendants.

🐞🐞🐞 Descendants are defined to be biological or legally adopted children. Step children are not descendants. If you want step children included in your estate planning, you must make explicit provisions for their inclusion.

There are several documents that are usually associated, and prepared, with the will:
1. Power of attorney
2. Durable power of attorney for health care
3. Declaration as to medical or surgical treatment
4. Burial/cremation instructions
5. Gift under Uniform Anatomical Gift Act (organ donation, if desired)
6. Tangible property list
7. Letters to the executor and beneficiaries stating wishes

An *advance health care directive*, also known as a **living will**, **personal directive**, **advance directive**, or **advance decision**, is a legal document in which a person specifies whether or not they wish to be given life-sustaining treatments or be administered artificial nourishment and hydration if they are no longer able to make decisions for themselves because of illness or incapacity. It may also include other medical directions that impact end of life and be accompanied by the specification of a durable power of attorney for health care decisions.

🐞🐞 There is now a Dementia Advance Directive available at www.dementia-directive.org.

👓👓👓 There are other documents that may exist such as a *Do Not Resuscitate* (DNR) order. A DNR does not withhold any treatment other than that which would require intubation, cardiopulmonary resuscitation (CPR), or Advanced Cardiac Life Support (ACLS). A DNR is the legal document that states that the person does not wish to receive resuscitative treatment if their heart were to stop or they were to stop breathing. This document is honored in medical facilities where it is on record, as well as in a home where the DNR is clearly posted. The order may not be honored if the emergency arises in a public place and the legal document is not present.

Considerations in making the decision to sign a DNR are
1. Resuscitation may prohibit natural death.
2. CPR is not effective in most people over the age of 70.
3. Most cases for seniors result in broken ribs and other significant damage.

A person having signed a DNR can temporarily suspend the DNR, via the appropriate presurgical document, for a predetermined time following a major surgery so that any cardiopulmonary difficulty that is assumed to be a temporary surgical byproduct can be addressed and corrected.

I prefer to think of a DNR as Death from Natural Reasons.

Trusts
A trust is a document that identifies the management of assets put into the trust. The trust is empty until it is funded by transferring your assets from you to the trust. This is done by changing the title of your assets from your individual

name to the name of the trust. Assets including real estate, bank accounts, investments, business interests, and notes payable to you can be put into a trust. A trust can be funded upon death by naming the trust as a beneficiary of an asset. (See Beneficiary Designation below.)

There are many types of trusts. The major types involved in estate planning are discussed below.

Trusts are either *revocable* or *irrevocable*. A **revocable trust** can be changed by the grantor, who is the creator, at any time in any way. An **irrevocable trust** typically does not allow changes of any kind by anyone.

A **living trust** is a trust that is in effect while the creator of the trust is alive. It is a revocable trust which can be changed by the creator at any time. Once the creator has deceased, it is no longer a living trust and is simply a trust. A living trust has a trustee, usually the creator, who manages the trust. A living trust offers five benefits:

1. Privacy
    Wills are filed with the county upon death, making all distributions and ownership public. Trusts are not filed with the county, and therefore ownership of the assets in the trust and the resultant asset distributions are not public. In some situations, registration of the trust may be required.

2. Probate avoidance
    The successor trustee does not have to file with the probate court to execute the distribution of assets as specified in the trust document. If the trust has been properly funded, meaning all large assets are in the name

of the trust or moved to the trust upon death (TOD), probate theoretically can be avoided.

👀 👀 👀 There are usually items that are not in a trust, and therefore a will is always needed.

3. Creditor protection
   The assets in an irrevocable trust created by the living trust for the beneficiary are protected from creditors if distribution requirements are specified. The use of a spendthrift clause exempts the inheritance from any previously "promised" creditors. Discuss with your lawyer and financial planner, the merits of creating an irrevocable trust for a beneficiary. An irrevocable trust will protect the beneficiary in case they divorce. It also could prevent assets from going into the beneficiary's estate for estate tax purposes. Also discuss the ramifications of generation skipping.

4. Control
   Restricted rather than outright distributions of assets can be designated via the creation of an irrevocable trust - see definition below.

5. Incapacity planning
   If the trustee becomes incapacitated, the successor trustee can oversee the trust without court intervention. Because a living trust is revocable, the trustee can legally dispute any claim that they are incapacitated and retain control of the trust.

With a living trust, the assets are individual assets and the trust owner pays an individual tax rate on income during their life.

A living trust can be a *joint trust*, listing more than one person as co-creator and co-trustee, usually spouses. When a co-owner of a joint trust is deceased, the surviving co-owner becomes the sole trustee.

The terms of a living trust supersede, take precedence over, the terms of a will in regard to property distribution for assets titled in the name of the trust. The living trust does **not** supersede tenancy or beneficiary designation (see below). All property in the living trust is controlled by the terms of the living trust and is not subject to the terms of a will.

Beneficiary trusts, created upon the death of the benefactor, are always irrevocable and typically cannot be changed. When created by a living trust, the beneficiary trust is known simply as an irrevocable trust, and when created by a will it is called a *testamentary trust*.

Irrevocable trusts not created as the result of the death of a benefactor are instead set up inter-vivos, meaning by a grantor while alive. The grantor gives up all ownership rights the moment they contribute assets to the trust.

Establishing an irrevocable trust for assets passed on to a beneficiary allows the decedent to place rules for distribution of the assets. This is particularly helpful in the case of a beneficiary who is either a minor, young adult or a less-than-responsible adult. For example, it is possible to establish that only income earned, if any, on the assets be distributed each year until a specific event has occurred, such as reaching a certain age, date, or life milestone. After that event, the beneficiary may take a partial or full distribution. Another option is to specify distributions for medical, housing and educational expenses only.

An irrevocable trust must be managed by a trustee. The living trust can identify the trustee for the irrevocable trust. If it does not, and the beneficiary has not been given the power to choose, the beneficiary can ask the court to be allowed to choose the trustee, otherwise the court will assign a trustee. Banks and investment companies, such as Schwab, have departments that manage such trusts. There are also independent trustees that may be more personal and less costly.

🐞🐞🐞 The irrevocable trust will identify the terms of the distribution of the assets within the trust, which may include restrictions based on age, need and or events. *Income tax is due on all income earned and capital gains tax on all capital gains earned by the trust.* Therefore, upon the creation of the irrevocable trust, the beneficiary should contact the financial adviser currently managing the assets to discuss a strategy to avoid a large tax burden. The objective is to withdraw income as a distribution when allowed.

The irrevocable trust may identify a time at which the assets can be fully distributed. At that time, if the beneficiary chooses to dissolve the irrevocable trust, they should:

1. Consider any potential tax ramifications and consult a financial advisor.
2. Consider keeping their inherited assets segregated from any marital assets. Contact a lawyer to ensure that assets are not comingled and that your updated estate planning documents reflect your wishes for any previously inherited assets.

Tenancy

Assets that are held with multiple parties in a form of joint tenancy **are not subject to probate**. These assets are distributed to the other owners outright without restriction. Tenancy is the manner in which 1. real property (fixed property, principally land and buildings such as a residence) or 2. personal property (movable property; belongings exclusive of land and buildings) is owned by multiple parties and by which the passing of the property, upon death of a party, to the surviving parties is defined. There are three types of tenancy.

Joint tenancy allows two or more joint tenants to equally own the same property. The biggest benefit to joint tenancy is the *right of survivorship* that provides for a tenant's ownership to be transferred to the surviving owners upon their death. Joint tenancy is called *tenancy by the entirety* in some states.

Tenancy in common is a less restrictive form of ownership than joint tenancy in several aspects. *First*, tenancy in common does not require the tenants to have equal ownership of the property. *Second*, the tenant is free of the restrictions for disposal of the property placed on them with the right of survivorship component of joint tenancy, therefore allowing a deceased tenant's ownership to go to an heir as opposed to a co-tenant.

Beneficiary Designation

A beneficiary designation allows the owner of an asset to specify the distribution of that asset upon their death. A named beneficiary may be an individual or a trust. The type of asset will determine the exact terminology used to specify the beneficiary. Some assets such as investments, life insurance and retirement assets allow the beneficiary or beneficiaries to be named as individuals. Other assets such as real estate deeds require that it be specified as transfer on death (TOD). Bank accounts specify that the asset be payable on death (POD). These assets are distributed to the beneficiary outright and without restriction. If assets are distributed, transferred or paid to a living trust, they then are under the terms of the living trust. Assets that allow for a named beneficiary designation **are not subject to probate.**

Small-Estate Affidavit
A small-estate affidavit is a document that is used to transfer property from a small estate (qualifying estate value defined per state), not in a trust, without having to go through probate. There are situations in which a small-estate affidavit **cannot** be used, including:
1. Proceedings for regular probate have already begun.
2. The estate is over the value limit for small estates. (check on the current value limit in your state)
3. Transfers of real estate are involved. Many states are now implementing special affidavits for transfers of real estate.

For an estate that has a trust containing the majority of owner assets, small-estate affidavits are used for assets left out of the trust, either intentionally or as an oversight, such as vehicles and other titled items for which it is not desirable to be titled in the name of the trust. Using a small-estate affidavit avoids having to go through probate to dispense with the titled items.

A small-estate affidavit can be downloaded from a court website. The signer then swears that they have the authority to dispense with the item, *and they become personally liable to do the right thing with the asset.* If the item is a vehicle, the seller will have to provide the purchaser with the small-estate affidavit and a copy of the death certificate at the time of purchase so that the purchaser can have the vehicle retitled.

Federal Estate Tax

Your estate, consisting of your money and property, may also be subject to federal estate tax after death. In 2018 the estate tax exclusion was $11.18 million per person, $22.36 million per couple. Anything over the estate tax exclusion is federally taxable at 40%. The tax law allows for permanent portability between spouses. This allows a surviving spouse to take advantage of any unused estate and gift tax exemption left by the deceased spouse. In addition, some states have an estate tax.

The portability option must be selected *when the estate tax return of the deceased spouse is filed, even if no federal estate tax is owed*. IRS Form 706 is used to preserve the unused portion of the decedent's estate tax exemption for their spouse. Check with your accountant to identify current tax laws.

Preparation allows a smooth transition for those who continue to live.
Trish Laub

Chapter 3

PREPARATION FOR THE END OF LIFE ...
what to do as the end approaches

No one wants to talk about the end of life. However, the more that it can be talked about, the easier it is to provide the end of life that is desired. The sooner the conversation can be started, the easier it will be, especially if it can take place prior to any medical crisis, life-limiting diagnosis or the approach of death. It is important to determine whether or not the person has embarked on estate planning. You can open the door to the conversation by simply asking a question, such as "Have you done any estate planning?" or "Do you have a will?" If they are receptive to your questions and have begun planning, ask where the documents are. If they have not begun planning, encourage the them to start. You can continue with more detailed questions: "Do you have any end of life wishes?", "Do you want to participate in end of life planning (such as writing an obituary)?" and "Have you completed the Five Wishes?" Be sure that you have answers to as many of the things that require decisions discussed in Chapter 6 as possible. If your questions are not met with receptivity, respect that and know that you may have to make decisions for them that may be hard for you.

There are specific things that should be done as each stage of the end of life approaches. Paying attention to these details will allow you to be prepared and able to participate fully in the end of life process.

What to Do as Far in Advance of Death as Possible

1. Assist with the creation of the Sections/Folders identified in the Afterword and complete any information that is incomplete. Be sure that originals of all necessary documents are available: legal, titles, etc.

2. Become familiar with the information in the Sections/Folders.

3. If the person has chosen to donate organs, contact the Organ Procurement Organization in your state. You can locate it at www.aopo.org/find-your-opo or call 703-556-4242. Also, if your loved one is receiving in-home hospice, let your hospice RN (Registered Nurse) know about the desire for organ donation. If they are in a hospital, notify the doctor and RNs. For information about organ donation, visit www.organdonor.gov.

What to Do Prior to Imminent Death

1. 🐞 🐞 🐞 Prior to death, if possible, the power of attorney should consider transferring cash into an estate account that the designated executor will have immediate access to after the anticipated death. The account can be set up to allow a financial planner to transfer assets. This is also helpful so that the executor can immediately use the funds to pay mortuary expenses, etc. Otherwise, the executor must go through probate and wait to acquire a letters testamentary to be allowed to access the funds. This may prevent the executor from doing their job in a timely manner. The alternative would be to transfer some cash into the designated executor's personal

account for use in closing the estate. There are expenses, such as burial/cremation, that are often significant and must be paid very soon after death.

🐞🐞 Any funds put into the executor's personal account legally become the property of the executor. Assuming that the executor is trusted, it can be agreed upon that they will distribute any funds not spent on estate settlement as designated by the will.

🐞🐞 For any joint account with a non-executor co-owner, the funds legally become the property of the co-owner upon the other owner's death. If the joint account includes an executor co-owner, the account is considered an estate account and it does not become the property of the executor upon the other owner's death.

2. Be aware of any upcoming appointments that must be canceled.

3. Be aware of any caregiver, medical or home health services scheduled.

4. Have the information necessary for the creation of the death certificate complete and available. (See the Afterword, Section/Folder I: General Information.)

5. If a decision has been made regarding which business (mortuary, cremation service) will be used, have that information available.

🐞🐞🐞 Upon death, power of attorney rights are terminated and either the executor (identified in the will) and/or the trustee (if a living trust exists) should proceed as described below.

What to Do at the Time of Death and Immediately Following

1. If the deceased had hospice services, notify the hospice RN or case manager. They can notify the appropriate coroner, mortuary and Social Security. If the deceased did not have hospice services, notify the coroner (for the county in which the deceased resided) and then <u>notify the mortuary and Social Security</u> **immediately**.

     Family members appreciate the opportunity to pay their last respects to the deceased prior to removal of the body from the home or facility.

2.   Be sure any valuable items, such as jewelry, have been removed from the deceased.

3. Notify family and close friends, as well as any caregivers.

What to Do the Day of or Day Following the Death

1. Cancel any upcoming appointments. (doctors, dentists, hair, nails, etc.)

2. Cancel any caregivers or home health services.

3. The executor and/or trustee are responsible for executing the final disposition wishes of the decedent. They should contact the mortuary/cremation service that will be handling the burial/cremation and schedule an appointment to discuss the details.

     At that meeting be sure to request at least <u>10 copies of the death certificate</u>, which will take several days. Once they have been received, <u>verify the information printed on the certificate</u> and make any necessary corrections immediately. The death certificate MUST be accurate. In addition, only originals of the death certificate are valid, copies are not.

4. Notify any other family, friends, business associates, and professionals utilized by the decedent that were not notified previously including: pastor, executor, attorney, accountant, financial advisor, insurance agent, employer, retirement plan, Dept. of Veterans Affairs, Social Security, Medicare or Medicaid, bank, physicians, hair stylist/nail tech, others (See the Afterword, Section/Folder I.)

5. Identify all bills that will need to be kept current such as mortgage or rent and utilities.

What to Do as Soon as Possible After the Death
The executor and/or trustee is in charge of keeping estate property safe during the settlement of the estate.

The executor and/or trustee should:
1. Schedule an appointment with the decedent's lawyer, financial advisor and accountant, in that order.

2. Obtain a copy of the decedent's will and any living trusts.

3. Obtain several originals of the decedent's death certificate from the funeral home.

4. Notify homeowner's insurance carrier if real estate is unoccupied.

5. Notify post office of where to forward decedent's mail, if appropriate.

The executor and/or trustee must <u>keep track of all time and expenses</u> incurred during settlement of the estate. The estate must compensate the executor and/or trustee for their eligible services. Some states allow for payment according to a formula plus expenses. Other states post compensation rates. Contact a lawyer or financial advisor for information on compensation in your state.

See Chapter 7 for details of estate settlement.

Hospice Matters.
The end of life
deserves as much
beauty, care and respect
as the beginning.
Unknown

Chapter 4

PROVIDING COMFORT CARE ...
palliative and hospice care

Several times when my mom was in the hospital a nurse would casually mention that Mom qualified for palliative care services. We were told that the purpose of palliative care was to provide comfort for the patient. Honestly, we didn't really understand what the service could provide for Mom, and we were too caught up in the crisis to stop to ask or try to understand. We knew that we were providing Mom with what we believed was everything she could need at home to be comfortable. It was not until about two weeks prior to my dad's passing that my family initiated hospice services for Dad. We understood that hospice services provided support and care during the end of life process, but beyond that we really didn't understand that service either.

In short, what we found is that hospice, in fact a subservice of palliative care, was one of the most important factors in facilitating their passing without pain and with the greatest possible peace. It was not until my friend's husband was again faced with cancer that I learned the value of the full umbrella of palliative care services.

🐞 🐞 🐞 Palliative care is often treated like a referral to any other specialist and may be covered by private insurance, Medicare, or Medicaid. Medicare covers hospice services provided by a Medicare-certified provider, as long as the patient qualifies for those services. Medicare benefit periods apply to hospice services, in the same way as they do for all other services. Some Medigap plans cover hospice care.

Medicaid benefits are determined by each state, but each is required to cover certain mandatory benefits and is allowed to add other optional benefits. Check with your insurance provider to determine your coverage for these services.

🐞🐞 This section is specific to palliative and hospice care as they relate to severe illness, life limiting or threatening disease and end of life. Other services such as skilled nursing, skilled rehab and home health services also are valuable. These are discussed in *Through the Rabbit Hole*.

The National Hospice and Palliative Care Organization is a great reference for information: www.nhpco.org.

What are Palliative and Hospice Care?

I believe that palliative care and hospice care are among the most misunderstood and most valuable services offered in medicine. These beneficial approaches are surrounded by myth and misinformation. Palliative care is an umbrella of comfort and quality of life care under which hospice care falls. <u>Palliative care is **not only** end-of-life care! It is beneficial even when cure is the goal.</u> When the end of life approaches and is inevitable, and no further curative treatments are being pursued, hospice care provides comfort though end of life.

Palliative Care

🐞🐞🐞 Again, palliative care is **not only** end-of-life care. It is helpful anytime during the course of an illness that is considered life limiting.

The National Hospice and Palliative Care Organization uses the National Consensus Project's definition of palliative care:

"palliative care is patient and family-centered care that optimizes the quality of life by anticipating, preventing and treating suffering." Palliative care throughout the continuum of illness involves addressing physical, intellectual, emotional, social and spiritual needs and facilitates patient autonomy, access to information and choice.

The spectrum of medical health ranges between wellness and illness. Conceptually, there are four types of illness:
1. Non-acute - one that is non-life threatening, treatable and curable such as a cold or an infection that is responsive to antibiotics
2. Acute – one that has quickly become severe and dangerous such as appendicitis
3. Chronic – one that persists for a long time, usually disease-based such as heart failure or chronic obstructive pulmonary disease
4. Life limiting (not terminally ill) or life threatening (symptomatic with possible recovery) illness – such as cancer

The misunderstanding of palliative care causes many to shy away from the services, afraid that use of them implies that the person is nearing death. That is **not** true. When patients improve, they may discontinue palliative care services unless and until they need them again in the future.

The umbrella of palliative care begins at the diagnosis of chronic, life limiting or life threatening illness - in short, life-altering illness. Palliative care providers are specialists in treating the symptoms of many types of disease, and therefore are an addition to your medical team. The focus of palliative care is on the patient's and their family's holistic care.

Palliative care is a valuable service even when cure is the goal, providing an additional layer of support for the patient, caregivers and family. The fact is it may even prolong life.

The final service offered under the palliative care umbrella is hospice care, which is specifically end-of-life care. It too, is a very misunderstood service that is discussed in the next section.

A palliative care team consists of highly skilled team members:

- Physicians, physician assistants (PA), and nurse practitioners (NP) representing palliative care, other specialties and primary care
- Advanced practice nurses (APNs), RNs
- Therapists: speech, physical and occupational, if needed.
- Child-life specialists
- Pharmacists
- Social workers
- Chaplains

The team is there to address:

- Symptom management of physical and emotional symptoms
- Psychological support
- Communication: clarification and coordination, assistance in decision-making
- Caregiver and family support
- End-of-life planning and referral to hospice

For further information regarding palliative care, call a local palliative care service and request a consultation. Google "palliative care" followed by your city and state.

Hospice Care

The focus of hospice care is end-of-life services. It is an invaluable service that provides comfort to <u>patients with terminal illnesses</u> who are <u>no longer continuing life-extending treatments</u>. The objective of hospice care is to provide a dignified and comfortable death among family and friends at home, although some circumstances require care in a hospice facility.

👀 👀 👀 Unless there is a reason the client needs to be cared for in a hospice facility, *hospice is intended to take place at home*. If the client's home situation is not suitable or in-home hospice is unable to manage the client's pain, a client may need to be cared for in a hospice facility.

As with palliative care, a hospice care team includes:

- The patient's primary care physician, PAs, and NPs
- Hospice physician (or medical director): the client may want the medical director to act as their primary care physician at this time
- Nurses: an RN will visit the client at least once a week, with the number of visits per week to be determined by the ongoing assessment of the client
- Home health aides: home health aides or CNAs (Certified Nursing Assistants) visit the client 1-3 times a week for a 1-2 hour session to include personal care, etc.
- Trained volunteers: visit to provide respite care for the family
- Pharmacists
- Social workers: visit initially and provide resources such as caregiver agencies
- Chaplains or other counselors: available on request for mental, emotional and spiritual needs

The team is there to provide:
- Pain and symptom management
- Assistance with the emotional, psychosocial and spiritual aspects of dying
- Medications related to the terminal diagnosis, medical supplies and durable equipment
- Education on how to care for the patient
- Short-term inpatient care when pain or symptoms become too difficult to manage at home
- Respite care
- Support and assistance at the time of death and following
- Bereavement counseling and care for surviving family and friends

What You Need to Know About Hospice
- 👀 👀 👀 Hospice <u>does **not** provide 24x7 caregivers.</u>

- <u>You do **not** have to discontinue all of your medications.</u> Hospice may recommend that the client does, but if there are medications that contribute to the quality of life, they may be continued.

- If a patient improves and no longer needs hospice services, they can discontinue the services. The patient can requalify for services if they are needed in the future.

- 👀 👀 👀 It takes several days for hospice supplies to arrive. *Plan on purchasing your own supplies to tide you over until those ordered by hospice arrive.*

For further information regarding hospice care, call a local hospice care service and request a consultation. Google "hospice care" followed by your city and state.

How are Palliative and Hospice Care Initiated for a Patient?

For both palliative and hospice care, a consultation can be requested by the patient's primary care physician or specialist, or the patient can make the request.

The consultation is used to provide information to the client about the services and also for the provider to verify the patient's eligibility for their services based on their health status. The consultation is conducted by a case manager or an RN. Once a patient has been found eligible, and has decided to proceed with a specific provider, a medical order is required to activate services. The chosen palliative or hospice provider will assign an RN as the case manager, who will conduct an assessment of the patient, identify their needs and create a care plan.

At some point early in the process a social worker will visit and provide additional information on resources that may be useful. You will also be contacted with an offer of assistance from clergy.

If at any time, and for any reason, the patient is not comfortable with the RN assigned to them, they may request another RN. It is incredibly important that the patient be comfortable with the RN who is coordinating the patient's care plan. The same is true for home health aides and CNAs.

Finding Palliative and Hospice Care

There are several ways in which you can find these services.

Palliative care is available at some hospitals, both as outpatient and inpatient, through outpatient clinics and as an in-home service. Hospice services are intended to be provided at home, although they may be administered in a hospice facility if the in-home environment is not suitable or pain management is not successful at home. Therefore, when looking for hospice, be sure to find one that either offers inpatient care or has a contract with a hospice that does.

Many hospitals offer palliative care services. If not, the hospital social workers should have recommendations of palliative care clinics and companies in your area. Some companies offer both palliative care and hospice services, providing a smooth transition between them. Other companies offer one or the other service. Start by asking your care provider or a trusted hospital for a recommendation. Next, Google "Palliative" or "Hospice" followed by your city and state.

Choose a palliative or hospice care provider that is certified in the field. The Joint Commission on Accreditation of Healthcare Organizations oversees the certification of palliative care programs in hospitals. The National Hospice and Palliative Care Organization is dedicated to leading and mobilizing social change for improved care at the end of life. Both organizations can provide helpful information on selection of a provider.

What You Need for In-Home Hospice

In-home hospice will provide any medications covered by the service, any durable equipment (hospital bed, walker, wheel chair) and any supplies (wipes, gloves, bed pads) needed. It will also identify how many times a week the RN will visit, as well as how many times per week a CNA will visit. RN visits are initially once per week and may increase as needed. CNA visits are two to three times per week and usually last a maximum of two hours. During that time the CNA assists with activities of daily living such as showering and grooming.

The RN will visit within 48 hours of bringing your loved one home from the hospital. During that visit, the nurse will provide you with any supplies that she may have on hand. You likely will need supplies before that, especially if you have not been providing in-home care. It will take several days after the RN's initial supply order has been placed for you to receive them.

Below is a list of items that you may find helpful in providing care. Those highlighted are possibly provided by hospice care, so you might want to purchase a small quantity of it until you know for sure.

Usually provided by hospice

🐞 🐞 🐞 Be sure to have some of the following, specific to your needs, prior to receiving your hospice supply order.

- Tabbed adult briefs (diapers)
- Liners/pads for the tabbed adult briefs
- Baby wipes
- Barrier wipes/paste

- Chux – disposable bed pads
- Nitrile (non latex) gloves – probably large

Durable medical equipment, as defined and approved by Medicare, can withstand repeated use and is:
- Used for a medical reason
- Not usually useful to someone who isn't sick or injured
- Used in your home
- Expected to last at least three years

This includes equipment such as wheelchairs, walkers, shower and transfer benches, commodes, pressure pads, air mattresses, hospital beds and bedside tray tables. It is really helpful to caregivers for the hospital bed to be adjustable not only at the head and foot of the bed, but also in the height from the floor.

Hospice can also order the equipment necessary for oxygen to be administered as well as any other medical devices.

Other items you might want to have
This list will vary with the needs of the person receiving hospice care.
- Face masks, to prevent the spread of germs
- Bar soap, not antibacterial soft soap, for disinfection
- Lotion, for the skin
- Personal wipes, usually around 8"x10", for personal clean up
- Hydrogen peroxide, to clean items and to clean up blood
- Rubbing alcohol, to clean items
- Antifungal powder, such as Desenex, will eliminate and deter heat rash anywhere that the skin touches itself
- Any special food items such as Ensure, juice, Jello

- A bell, for the patient to ring for assistance
- Baby wipes
- Baby wipe warmer, to take the chill off of cold baby wipes
- One Drop, used in a toilet or commode to effectively reduce odor
- Hospital bed sheets, which are longer than regular twin sheets
- Straight bed sheet, twin or full, to use when moving the patient
- Reusable, washable bed pads, to prevent the bed from getting wet or soiled
- Goodnights disposable adhesive bed pads, to prevent the bed from getting wet or soiled
- Motion monitor, to know if the patient is out of bed
- Baby monitor, to hear the patient
- Garbage bags, to dispose of everything that is unsanitary
- Shelving, to consolidate supplies for convenient access
- Desk floor mat, to place under a commode to protect the floor
- Bed tray table, for eating, reading and grooming
- A foam roller, approximately 5-6 inches in diameter, to place at the end of the bed under the sheets to keep the sheets from drawing back on the patient's toes

Several of the items listed above can be purchased at a medical supply store, however they can usually be found at less cost online including on amazon.com, and at stores such as Walgreens, Target, and Bed Bath & Beyond.

You may find that, due to your circumstances, you need additional supplies. See *Through the Rabbit Hole* for more information regarding durable medical equipment, assistive devices and helpful medical supplies needed for care.

🐞🐞 If the person receiving in-home hospice care has been in the hospital, always bring home all supplies in the hospital room when the patient is discharged. This might include any buckets used for bathing, gloves, bed pads, barrier cream, antifungal powder, Kleenex, etc. It has all been charged to the patient and is therefore their's to take home.

How soon will we get medications, medical supplies and equipment?

Hospice furnishes some medications, medical supplies and equipment. There are two types of medication that are dispensed by hospice care. First, hospice care will provide a set of medications that are to be kept at the home for use in managing some of the symptoms of end of life, such as pain, anxiety and difficulty breathing. Second, some of the patient's current medications, those necessary for the client's comfort and quality of life, are provided by hospice, such as blood pressure medication. The delivery of the first order of medications can take a day or longer, as the prescriptions must be approved by the hospice pharmacy. After the initial order, medications are often delivered within hours.

Medical equipment is usually delivered within 24 hours. If the hospice provider has its own medical-equipment supplier, delivery may be sooner. Durable equipment such as hospital beds and commodes must be delivered before a patient can be brought home from the hospital.

🐞🐞🐞 It can take up to several days for supplies to be delivered, especially if the delivery window spans a weekend. Therefore, plan on purchasing some supplies of your own to be used before your hospice order is delivered. (See the previous section for a list of supplies to have on hand.)

It's the gradual unraveling of a life,
and a slow and gentle letting-go."
Felicity Warner

Chapter 5

THE FINAL STRETCH ...
the walk home

It is the greatest privilege to accompany someone on their final walk home. I have been given this privilege several times and have found it to be an opportunity to truly express love for another. But, it is not for everyone. Some want to actively participate during the transition while others want to be present only before or after the process is complete. Every person has different thoughts on if and how they want to be present. There is no right or wrong, it is individual.

> Energy cannot be created or destroyed,
> it can only be changed
> from one form to another.
> Albert Einstein

No matter your belief system, the first law of thermodynamics states that energy cannot be created or destroyed. Therefore, what we perceive as a process of death is really a transition from one form of energy to another. And because of this, we must tend to the energy until the process is complete.

Creating the Transition Space
During the final stretch of the transition process, as the soul prepares to release its use of the body, the emphasis shifts from physical care to care for the spirit.

The physical location where the transition will take place may be in a home or a facility. A transition space is the place where life on earth and the energy of the spirit separate, and can be created anywhere. The objective is to create a space that is tranquil, giving consideration to light, sound, color, smell and possibly access to nature. It should be a dedicated, if only temporarily, space that is clean, calm and clutter free or at least organized.

When my in-laws were bringing my mother-in-law back to her home, their first thought was to create a space in their dining room. It was a practical thought, but upon further consideration they opted for creating a space in their family room, which overlooked the patio and the huge tree she sat under every summer evening for decades. The benefit of her being able to look outside and to feel the afternoon sun on her skin outweighed any practicality offered by the dining room. While the dining room was more separated from the rest of the house, offering one kind of privacy, the family room also offered a physical door for privacy.

A friend, when faced with the future death of her spouse and understanding that he wanted his transition space to be at home, asked me if he would die in their bed. I asked her if that is what she wanted. The answer was not important to me; it was important that she considered it and could then discuss it with her husband. I assured her that any setup was possible in their home.

As a facilitator of the transition, you have multiple roles through which you can ensure comfort and dignity.

First, you can continue to maintain the tranquility of the environment. If the patient has stated preferences or made specific requests in estate planning documents, Five Wishes (see Afterword) or during a previous conversation, follow those requests. Here are some suggested alternatives:

- Promote and allow only positive energy in the space.
- Use soft lighting and soothing sounds.
- Incorporate color as a way to provide comfort. Favorite colors evoke childhood and positive memories, blues can be calming, and yellows and oranges can energize.
- Bring nature, possibly flowers, indoors or take the person to a window or outside when possible.
- Incorporate personal photos, cards and comfort.
- Use items that are soft and provide comfort such as lightweight fleece blankets, soft clothing or pajamas and a soft stuffed animal.

As caregiver for the spirit you should:

- Address them directly using whatever name they are used to hearing from you: Mom, Dad, Papa, honey, etc.
- Sit in silence, or meditate, to bring peace to the person and the space.
- Synchronize your breathing with their's if they appear to be distressed or their breathing changes. Possibly put their hand on your heart and ask them to breathe with you. This can be done even if they are not awake.
- Reassure and affirm without judgment, especially if there are life regrets, and honor and support their spirit.
- Change bed linens and pajamas often. The body and bed should never be dirty.
- Continue grooming such as brushing their hair and cleaning their teeth when possible. Continue body baths as long as it does not cause discomfort.
- Be sure that they are never wet or soiled. It is important not to let the skin deteriorate. The use of barrier cream may be necessary.

- Use a warm cloth on the face, eyes, hands and feet frequently. The warmth alone is comforting.
- Continue to moisten the lips and to use lip balm as often as necessary.
- Change their position at least every two hours. It is very important to continue this as long as possible. Close to transition it may be possible only to change the position of the head and shoulders. Adjustments should be done very slowly and gently. Any movement may be uncomfortable at this point.
- Check that the ears are flat, not crimped under the head. This can not only be uncomfortable but can also minimize hearing and inhibit circulation.

👀 👀 My personal preference when facilitating a transition is to allow the spouse to continue the role of spouse as opposed to primary caregiver. In other words, let the spouse be with the person in transition, without fulfilling any responsibilities. The spouse of someone in transition may want to be part of the caregiving team, and that is to be respected. I explain that the spouse has a purpose that only they can fulfill, no one else, which is to provide the comfort and love of a spouse. Once stated, it is up to the spouse to determine what their role will be in the process. Every person, every relationship, and generational norms and expectations are different. All are to be respected.

Be aware of the process of the senses.
- Vision is the first sense to diminish, and peripheral vision is the first to fail. Therefore, when you enter the room stand at the end of the bed so that you can be seen. Once they know that you are there, you can move around. Also, as their earthly vision diminishes you may perceive that they can see another dimension that we

78

cannot, one containing loved ones who have passed before.

- Smell is a sense that instantaneously brings back memories. Like the presence of color, scents can affect mood and emotion. The benefit of smell is that it can be effective even after the person is no longer seeing or opening their eyes. It is thought that smelling through the left nostril evokes positive emotions while smell through the right nostril is more negative. Scents can be sprayed lightly onto a pillowcase and diluted essential oils can be applied to the body. While lavender is soothing, the most enjoyed scent is vanilla. Always ask for permission to use scents and determine what scents the person in transition enjoys.

- Touch often intensifies before it diminishes. Therefore, be gentle. Start with gently putting cream on their hands and feet. If that is comfortable you can offer massage with very light pressure. The body at this point is delicate and requires extreme care.

- Hearing is last to go, but speak gently and distinctly, using few words. Always tell them what you are doing and continue to ask for permission before touching them. If you leave the room, tell them you will be back, even if they are not conscious. People in comas have reported hearing everything that was said near them.

🐞 🐞 🐞 In an effort to do everything possible to provide comfort during the transition, as their liquid intake decreases, it is tempting to want to use IV hydration. Always check with your medical provider and/or hospice RN, but more often than not it is not a good choice. If the body's need for liquid and its ability to eliminate it is decreasing, artificially adding liquid can cause swelling and bloating, which can become not only uncomfortable and visually distressing but also counterproductive.

As the spirit prepares to leave the body, remove all stimulation by dimming lights and reducing sound. Give them permission to leave, assure them that those of us left behind will be fine, tell them that they will always be loved and that their life was meaningful, and let them know that they will be safe after they transition.

> You took my hand and I fell asleep.
> Felicity Warner

The greatest gift you can give a spirit is to be there for it as it leaves its body behind and exits the world we know. In *A Safe Journey Home, A Simple Guide to Achieving a Peaceful Death,* Felicity Warner details the process of a soul midwifing a spirit through transition.

How to Know the End is Approaching
The process of transitioning from life is as individual as the person, making it incredibly difficult to determine the exact steps that will accompany the transition. The fact that the cause for the transition can vary so greatly adds to the difficulty. Following are some steps that you may or may not witness.

Often the process consciously begins with the person changing from an outer focus, including visitors and external stimuli, to an inner focus with a withdrawal from the world.

Usually 1 month or less prior to transition, they will begin to process their life, having their eyes closed and increasing sleep. Verbal communication may decrease creating a greater value to wordlessness and touch. Things associated with the physical body, such as appetite, may become unimportant and that is okay. Mental and physical changes, more so than those related to a specific medical condition, usually begin 1 to 2 weeks prior to transition. Sleeping becomes almost constant, but they can be awakened, as they seem to have one foot in each of two worlds. They may indicate the presence of loved ones who have passed before them. Disorientation and agitation, such as picking at blankets and clothes, might be the response – at some level – to moving between the two worlds. As the physical body begins to lose its ability to maintain itself, there may be physical changes such as:

- Lower blood pressure
- Very high or low pulse
- Variance in body temperature
- Increased perspiration
- Change in skin color and bluish color to the hands, feet, and nails due to lack of oxygen
- Chest congestion, sometimes rattling
- Breathing rate and rhythm changes

All of these symptoms can come and go, minute to minute.

Usually within a week of transition, often only days or hours prior, there is what I call the rally, a burst of energy as though the person is going to recover. They may be clear and alert, have an appetite for their favorite foods, and want to be social. It is as though they have received a new form of energy, that which will carry them through their transition. Shortly after the rally, you may begin to see signs of symptoms of damage to the body caused by the final stages of disease or the beginning of the organs shutting down, such as swelling and bloating.

In addition, during this time there may be a moment during which, in retrospect, you thought that the person had made the decision to "just be done." Often after that the person mostly sleeps, and is initially responsive to assistance but is later nonresponsive. After this time, intake of food and liquid is minimal, if at all.

1 to 2 days to hours prior to transition, the symptoms that recently appeared will intensify, in particular:
- Restlessness
- Breathing patterns, with breaths stopping for 10-20 seconds
- Congestion gets very loud, with a rattling quality
- Open or semi-open eyes that are not seeing, look glassy, and often tear
- Elimination of bodily fluids and waste, which may contain blood
- Purple color to hands and feet, blotches at the joints, and eventually blood pooling, called mottling, at the lowest points under the arms and legs
- Non-responsiveness

👀 👀 My dad had a pacemaker and, as the transition process progressed, I became afraid that it would not allow him to let go. We expressed our concern with our hospice provider who could then take appropriate action.

Prior to the final breaths, there is often almost a gasping, like a fish out of water. Then there can be what appears to be *the final breath, which can be followed by one or two long spaced breaths.* They no longer have use for their now cumbersome body. <u>When breathing has stopped and there is no pulse, the process is complete.</u>

Each person's end-of-life process is unique. Sometimes it may appear that the person is waiting for something prior to transitioning. It may be the resolution of a regret or relationship, a visit from someone important to them, or an upcoming event such as an anniversary. I know people who have called family members into town to provide the opportunity for peace for their loved one, and others who have celebrated an event before the actual date. Some people prefer to pass surrounded by their loved ones, other's enjoy the almost party-like gathering of loved ones and will only pass when everyone has left them alone. The most difficult situation may be when the person appears to be resisting transition due to fear. In that case, continually reassure them that they are safe and loved, and that their life was meaningful.

If you have the privilege of overseeing or participating in the end-of-life process, you can help make the process as pleasant and peaceful as possible. Stay in touch with your hospice RN, or the RN in a facility, in order to keep the person comfortable, ease their breathing, and keep them pain free with the use of sublingual medication administered under the tongue or in the side of the cheek.

And, continue to: (See Creating a Transition Space above.)
- Keep the environment positive and peaceful, possibly using gentle lighting and peaceful or favorite music.
- Care for the body, keeping it clean and moving the body every 2 hours.
- Keep the bed clean and fresh.

- Talk to the person, they can hear until their final breath.
- Reinforce that they are safe and loved.
- Consider celebrating a near future important event if you suspect that they are waiting for the celebration.
- If there is fear involved, continue to reassure them that they will be safe after they transition.

Medical Aid in Dying

Recently, more states have begun to offer an end-of-life option known as medical aid in dying or death with dignity. It is available, based on specific requirements that provide checks and balances, for terminally ill and mentally capable adults who have a prognosis of six months or less to live. Those with dementia are ineligible. After meeting the requirements, a patient is prescribed life-ending medications that must be self-administered allowing for a peaceful death.

I have found that there are many misconceptions about these programs and strongly recommend that if interested, contact be made with a professional working with a program. In states where these programs are legal, medical facilities (hospitals, hospices, and private practices) may choose to opt-in to a program of this kind. A hospice who has opted in will be able to help facilitate a patient through this process. Ask your hospice program if they have opted in. A patient and family who access a medical aid in dying program may potentially face very specific needs in regard to their grief process.

Information regarding the status of this offering in each state can be found at www.deathwithdignity.org and additional information at www.compassionandchoices.org.

After a life has come to a close,
honoring the final wishes is the last step
in preserving the dignity of the life.
Trish Laub

Chapter 6

AFTER TRANSITION ...
disposition of the body, writings and gatherings

After transition is complete, another process of a practical nature begins. The body, the vessel for the spirit while on earth, must be properly tended to, and the decedent may be celebrated. The celebration may have one or many aspects, from writing an obituary and/or eulogy to hosting a gathering of friends and loved ones. It is the responsibility of the executor and/or trustee to see that the decedent's final wishes are executed.

Disposition of the Body
The process of tending to the body after the transition involves many decisions and can be expensive. Hopefully, the decedent made most of those decisions as part of their estate planning or in the specification of their final wishes.

Today, more people are moving toward cremation and celebration of life gatherings instead of burial and funerals. Any choice, or combination of choices, is acceptable. Know that there are now more options, incorporating creativity, as to what is done in honor of a loved one whose life has ended.

The time immediately following a loved one's transition is often overwhelming. The clearer you can be on what they wanted, the less likely you are to be convinced that something unwanted or unnecessary is needed. Although most funeral directors are ethical and in the business to help people, occasionally there are those who take advantage of people in a vulnerable state of mind.

Questions to be Answered
- Did the decedent want to be buried or cremated?
- How did they want to be buried or what did they want done with their cremated remains (cremains)?
- Who did they want notified?
- Did the decedent want a funeral service, memorial, or celebration of life?
- Did the decedent want an obituary? Did they write one?

If the decedent conveyed their wishes, then your job is a bit easier. If not, the executor, if specified, or spouse or next of kin will have to make those decisions. There are two things that must be considered in making those decisions: any religious beliefs and expense.

What to have Prepared
Information needed for the death certificate:
- Decedent's full legal name, maiden name
- Date and place of birth, gender
- Decedent's address including county
- Social Security number
- Father's name, place of birth, birth date
- Mother's maiden name, place of birth, birth date
- Marital status, spouse's full name
- Education (level)
- Occupation
- Military service, branch, years
- Date and place of death, age
- Manner and cause of death (natural, accident, illness)
- Method (burial, cremation), place of disposition

See the Afterword, Section/Folder I: General Information.

Information and decisions needed by the funeral director:
- Main contact name and means of contact
- Payment method: prepaid, cash, check, credit card, insurance assignment
- A recent photo, for identification
- Disposition of the body and final destination of body or cremains
- Cemetery if applicable
- Grave marker, if applicable, name and birth-death dates, inscriptions (can be simple), pictures, emblems, other detail
- Casket/vault/urn/cremation container selections: cemeteries require an outer receptacle for the casket at burial, crematories require a cremation container for placement of the body during cremation
- Viewing the body – public/private, open/closed, none
- Services/gatherings
- Clothing for the body, if desired, including undergarments, jewelry, eyeglasses, hair decorations, nail polish, cosmetics, etc. Is the regular hairdresser to be called?
  👓👓 Items such as eyeglasses, hearing aids, dentures, and pacemakers will be removed prior to cremation.
- Insurance policies
- Veteran's discharge papers (DD-214)
- Religious affiliation (if applicable)
- Pallbearers (if applicable) 6-8, plus honorary (who cannot carry casket)
- Readings: scriptures, poems, literary passages
- Music: favorite songs, musicians, vocalists
- Flowers and donations

- Gathering participants: celebrants, readers, musicians, etc. (if applicable)
- Programs, bookmarks
- Memorial table
- Video
- Post-gathering event: reception at home, restaurant, favorite place (event planner, organizer)
- Special notes to family

<u>Information helpful in creating an obituary</u>
See *Writings* section below for a detailed list of information useful in creating an obituary.

<u>For printed materials</u>
If you want printed materials such as memorial cards or bookmarks, you may want to select a religious verse or poem to include. Poems about grief can be found on most mortuary websites or Google "poems about grief" or "verses about death."

Options for Disposition of the Body
In 2018, I checked several mortuary websites offering both burial and cremation services. The dollar amounts stated in this section are based on that research. There is a significant difference in the cost of burial and cremation. There is a wide variance charged by mortuaries and cremation services. The following costs may vary by state, and will change over time, but are an example of the *relative cost difference* in services. The average cost for burial can range from $6,000-$10,000, the lower starting with burial only and the latter including funeral services and gatherings. The average cost for burial and a funeral was $8,300. Cremation costs range from $1,200 - $3,000, starting with the cost of cremation only and increasing with the addition of gatherings. You can go on

any mortuary or cremation service website to find current pricing as well as what services are included. It is well worth it to be clear on what services will be wanted and to check pricing in your area.

Even within a service the prices can vary greatly. That is why it is important to understand the options and to do your research prior to needing the services. Upon my dad's passing, my mom had decided that she wanted to use a specific mortuary and therefore my family did not do any research into alternatives. At that time, the selected mortuary did not offer cremation-specific packages. The mortuary charged us for their minimal burial package, of which we didn't use several additional services, and we were billed approximately $3,000 for cremation and the printing of bookmarks. In preparation for my mom's cremation, my family researched alternatives and found the Cremation Society for Colorado (there are others across the country) who charged us $900 for the same services. We did in fact write a letter to the ethics department of the mortuary we used for my dad, expressing that we felt that their practice had been unethical. We received acknowledgment but no restitution.

It is also important to understand that a mortuary traditionally works with burial but many have expanded to include cremation. There are independent cremation services that in many cases use the crematory of a mortuary. 👀👀 Another option is whole body donation for medical research and education. There is no cost for the donation or the subsequent cremation process and return of the cremains. (Google: anatomical donation and cremation.)

Burial and Cremation

Basic services offered for both simple burial and cremation are:

- 24-hour availability
- Transfer of the deceased from the place of death
- Basic staff services including consultation with the survivors and coordination of final destination
- Refrigeration, as needed
- Obtaining any permits necessary
- Preparation of the death certificates
  Be sure to order extra copies, possibly 5-10. They are needed in settling the estate. Copies of the death certificate will be available in 7-10 days. Also verify the final death certificate for accuracy and require corrections immediately.
- Notification to Social Security
  It is important that this be done **immediately**. The longer the Social Security number is active, the easier it is for it to be used for identity theft, which will make filing final taxes a nightmare. Call the funeral director a day or two later for verification that this has been done.
- Free online obituary
  A newspaper obituary can be placed for a minimal fee if you include only the decedent's full name, the birth and end-of-life dates, and a link to the online obituary.

Burial includes:
- An allowance for a basic casket may be included. If not, it is an additional expense and can range from $1,300 - $15,000.

Cremation includes:
- The cremation process performed in a casket or container at 1800 degrees Fahrenheit.

- A cremation container required by law for placement of the body during cremation. The most basic container is fiberboard. The cremation container is burned during the cremation.
- Verification of decedent's identity: to avoid error in the irreversible cremation process, every precaution is taken to ensure correct identification of the decedent prior to cremation. A family member may be asked to view and make a final identification of the deceased. If family members do not wish to do that, a current photograph of the decedent can suffice. A labeling device is used to identify the decedent, which may be a metal coin-like object with an identification number engraved on it. The device will go through the cremation process with the body and will stay in the human cremains.
- A basic urn, often a sturdy cardboard: this is most often used if price is an issue and/or if the cremains will eventually be scattered or used for another purpose.

Some mortuaries and cremation services will provide a digital keepsake of the decedent's fingerprint for free. Memorial cards and bookmarks can be purchased for an additional cost. Often a variety of keepsakes are available for purchase.

Embalming is necessary if there will be a viewing. There may also be an additional expense if an autopsy has been performed.

Additional cost, reflected in various packages of services, will be incurred for the addition of a funeral and other gatherings, as well as witnessing or previewing cremation.

Both services typically offer all of the types of gatherings for an additional fee. Gatherings can be customized to include almost anything that you might want such as food service and musicians.

In the event that <u>a decedent transitioned in a state other than where they will be buried</u>, a local mortuary must handle the necessary steps in order to transport the body to a funeral home in another state. For burial this is called a minimum transfer and involves transportation and preparation of the body (embalming), creation of the death certificates and provision of a temporary container for transportation. The family will have to pay the price of a plane ticket as though the decedent were a regular passenger, even though they will travel in the cargo section. Currently, that process costs between $1,000 (a cremation service)- $3,000 (a mortuary). If the decedent is cremated prior to transfer, the minimum transfer includes transportation, cremation and death certificates. There are then two options for transfer to the other state: via the United States Postal Service for approximately $100 or the cremains can be carried onto a flight for free. If the cremains are to be mailed, they must be marked specifically by the Post Office.

Special Considerations for Veterans
For complete information on Veterans Affairs (VA) benefits for deceased veterans go to www.cem.va.gov.

Active duty members, or veterans discharged under conditions other than dishonorable, are entitled to burial in a VA national cemetery. Space cannot be reserved in a VA national cemetery ahead of time and must be arranged for at the time of death, based on availability. Documentation, in the form of active duty identification or a DD-214 discharge form, is required to prove that the decedent qualifies for burial benefits.

Burial in a VA national cemetery includes:
- An assigned gravesite (if space is available)
- Opening and closing of the grave
- A grave liner for casketed remains
- A government headstone or marker
- Perpetual care at no cost to the family
- Cremains are buried or interred in VA national cemeteries in the same manner and with the same honors as casketed remains.

👀 👀 Not all expenses are covered. For example, the cost of a casket must be paid for by the family. Some mortuaries may offer discounts for non-covered items, provided to members of the American Legion and the Veterans of Foreign Wars.

A military funeral honors ceremony is available for all eligible veterans. The ceremony includes the folding and presentation of the United States flag and the playing of "taps," upon the family's request. The funeral director will request military funeral honors on behalf of the veteran's family. In addition, the family can request both a Presidential Memorial Certificate (via the VA office) and a folded American flag. The meaning of the flag folds is as follows:
- The first fold is a symbol of life
- The second fold is a symbol of our belief in eternal life
- The third fold is made in honor and remembrance of the veterans, departing their ranks who gave a portion of their lives for the defense of our country to attain peace throughout the world

Visit www.cem.va.gov for more information including information on the criteria for burial of spouses and family members in VA national cemeteries.

Options for Final Destination of the Body or Cremains
Burial:
- Earth Burial
- Above Ground Burial (Entombment)

Cremation:
- Earth burial
- Above Ground Burial (Entombment)
- Cremation garden or niche
- Memorial benches and pedestals
- Scattering (see following note) on earth or sent into space
- Keepsakes

🐞🐞 There are many options for scattering cremains. There are laws regarding where cremains can be legally spread. Scattering can happen all at once, or the cremains can be separated and spread in multiple places. The cremains may not appear as you would expect. They are **not** ash, but instead are made up of bone fragments and a heavy chalky component. If you try to spread them in the wind, you may get a mouth full. If you try to spread them in water, they will not float nicely but instead will sink to the bottom in a cement-like mass.

Today cremains can be sent into space with NASA or placed in a firework display, used to pot a plant or a tree, or even incorporated into keepsakes such as personal urns, picture frames, jewelry including diamonds, and hand-blown glass globes. The options are truly limitless.

Writings

There are two types of writings that may be used to honor the decedent: an obituary and a eulogy. An obituary typically appears in the local newspaper, if only to reference the actual obituary which appears on a mortuary or cremation service website. A eulogy is part of a gathering, and is most often spoken.

Although it may be difficult, it is helpful when your loved one, their spouse and/or family can do some preparation of these writings. One suggestion is to request that family members write a letter to the person who is approaching end of life, so that they can enjoy them while they are alive. These letters often become useful while creating an obituary as well as a eulogy. Getting a start on the outline of an obituary or eulogy is helpful as it is much more difficult to do it while grieving.

Obituary

An obituary can easily be created by incorporating a few facts and adding a photo. At the top of the obituary, list the full name and "birth – end-of-life" dates. Then write a couple of paragraphs including:

- Place of birth and youth
- Brief history of school and education
- Work history, career overview
- Passions
- Community service, military service or citations
- Organizations and memberships
- Special achievements and events
- Place of death
- Surviving relatives (step-relatives)

- Preceded in death by
- Religious information

Mortuaries often include writing an obituary in their services and independent businesses that offer end-of-life services will write an obituary for a fee.

Eulogy
A eulogy can include information in an obituary but usually includes more personal stories and memories. It can take almost any format that is desired including as a letter to the decedent.

Gatherings
There are a variety of gatherings that can be held to allow closure and support for both family and friends of the decedent. Gatherings can be included in a mortuary or cremation service package or they can be planned independently if the body is not going to be present, other than in a cremated form. You may find, depending on what you want, that you can organize a gathering on your own for less expense. For example, my family chose to do a celebration of life in my parents' home and prepared the food ourselves. I have attended gatherings that were catered in a family member's home and others in small venues serving coffee and cookies. The options really are unlimited.

The use of Caringbridge.com (see Chapter 1, Sharing Information) can be immensely helpful for posting information about gatherings, logistics and lodging for those coming from out of town; specification of charities for donations; and making provision for comments and condolences. It allows for the posting of a link to an obituary and the addition of videos. A trusted family member or friend can be asked to administer the page.

🐞🐞 If you choose to host a gathering at a location other than the home of the decedent, you might want to ask someone to stay in the home during the time of the gathering. Thieves sometimes look for the details of gatherings and use that time to commit thefts. It is also a consideration for close family members who will be attending the gathering.

Types of Gatherings
- Visitations, wakes, or viewings are usually held the day prior to a funeral and allow others to offer condolences to the family. Sometimes a private viewing for family only is held immediately prior to the funeral service.
- Funeral services are typically faith based and aim to provide closure.
- Memorial services or celebrations of life aim to honor the memories of the decedent without the body present.
- Military funeral honors ceremonies (See Special Considerations for Veterans above.)
- Graveside services are typically for family and close friends.

Gathering Considerations
- Will the body or cremains be present?
- Location?
- Will there a celebrant?
- Will pallbearers be needed?
- What personalization is wanted: photos, music, readings, poems or prayers?
- Will any personal custom or theme be incorporated?
- Will there be food and or drink?

Closure:
an often comforting or satisfying
sense of finality.
Merriam-Webster Dictionary

Chapter 7

SETTLING AN ESTATE ...
dotting the "i"s and crossing the "t"s

We learned the hard way. We thought that because my dad's will and trust both stated that my dad's assets and property were to become my mom's property, and because in several cases both of their names were already on the asset, that we didn't have to do anything. We were wrong. My dad passed away eight months prior to my mom. We did nothing to legally settle my dad's estate. When my mom passed away and her executor, my sister, began to settle her estate, we learned that she could not distribute Mom's assets because Dad's estate had not been settled. So, my sisters and I met with our parents' lawyer to identify how to first settle our dad's estate and then settle our mom's estate. Estate plans detail what is to happen with an estate upon death. *Legal action must be taken to translate those instructions into the legal distribution and transfer of assets, with proper title when necessary.*

Because our parents had estate plans, the distribution of their financial assets was specified. The largest task we faced was sorting through their personal property, which included personal property that had belonged to three of our grandparents. It was daunting to say the least. We fortunately came to a workable, tolerable strategy to handle a process that often breaks sibling relationships.

🐞🐞🐞 Even the smallest estate has to be settled, if only to file a death certificate. If there are assets, they must be distributed. <u>The estate has to be legally settled even if all</u>

assets are to go to a spouse: deeds and titles, account names and associated Social Security numbers must be changed.

🐞 🐞 Settling an estate can take months, even years, so it may be important to let any beneficiaries know that their distribution will not be made until all assets and liabilities have been settled. <u>Any assets to be inherited will be distributed last</u>.

What a Surviving Spouse has to Do
The details in Chapter 6 and the rest of this chapter are written for executors and apply to anyone who has died. There are several considerations for surviving spouses.

Even if all of the deceased spouse's assets are distributed via their will and/or living trust, the process of probate may be necessary to make the transfer of assets to the surviving spouse legal.

Other than actions required to settle the estate (transfer assets to the spouse), it is advisable *not to make any major decisions for one year.* Do not underestimate the shock that is experienced when a spouse is gone.

- Do not put your home on the market or sell your home. The possible exception is if capital gains on the sale is a concern. Contact a Financial Advisor/Planner.
- Do not gift or loan money to anyone.
- Don't impulsively spend money.
- Do not give personal property away until you are clear headed and can make good decisions. Do not let family or friends pressure you to make decisions before you are ready.
- Don't sell any investments, or purchase any new ones especially with the proceeds of an insurance policy.

Do, however, consider keeping joint bank accounts open for a period of time to allow for odd checks to clear and/or credits to come in.

While you need to wait a while to make certain decisions, there are several organizations you need to contact as soon as possible. Most are identified in the following chapter sections, however, it is worthwhile to mention the following in regard to surviving spouses.

- Check with the decedent's employer.
  - ○ Are there pension payments that will continue?
    There are typically two pension benefit options. One option is to take the maximum payment during the retired employee's life, and payments are discontinued upon their death. The other option, known as the joint and survivor benefit option, provides lower payments during the life of the retiree, but continues to make payments to the surviving spouse throughout the spouse's life. The pension option that may affect your payments had to be decided upon at the time your spouse signed up to receive payments.
  - ○ Is there a retirement or 401(k)/IRA plan? If so, those assets may be rolled into an account for the spouse's benefit if they were named beneficiary. Consult an accountant and a financial planner to determine the best way to handle the retirement benefit.
  - ○ Is health insurance available to the surviving spouse?
- Contact the life insurance company if the deceased had a policy.
  When you cancel a life insurance policy and make a claim for the benefits, you may be advised by the insurance company to let the company keep your proceeds in their money market fund. That may or may

not be the best option for you. It may be possible for you to instead receive monthly payments for life. Consult an accountant or financial planner before making any decision.

- 👀👀👀 Contact Social Security.
  - o As stated, it is critical to **immediately** notify Social Security of the spouse's death. This is to prevent identify theft, in this case the use of the Social Security number of someone who is deceased.
  - o Inquire about any death benefits and/or monthly benefits for which a spouse or family member may be eligible. These benefits must be applied for, sometimes within the month of death.
  - o Possibly on another call, at a slightly later date, contact Social Security to determine what your monthly payment will be. There are many different options in regard to Social Security payments. The spousal options that may affect your payments had to be decided upon at the time your spouse signed up to receive payments. Social Security can help identify those choices and how they impact your payments in the future.

Many times the surviving spouse finds themselves in uncharted financial waters. Spouses share responsibilities and often one spouse handles most of the financial decisions and responsibilities. If the surviving spouse is not comfortable with the financial aspects of their estate, they may want to put together a team consisting of a lawyer, accountant and financial planner (for this, consider a fee-only situation).

Hopefully a budget existed prior to the loss of the spouse. If not, a budget should be created to determine where the surviving spouse stands financially. The financial support team identified above can be instrumental in creating a new budget. Again consulting with the financial support team, determine the monthly income and the expenses, determine any necessary reserve (to be kept in a liquid account), and discretionary income if any. Sadly, surviving spouses often find themselves living on less money than before and an accurate picture of their financial situation is critical.

Finally, as soon as possible, the surviving spouse should review their will and any living trust to re-evaluate the power of attorneys, executors and trustees. Often spouses list each other for each of those responsibilities, and the surviving spouse may need to now list other relatives or friends. They also need to review all beneficiary designations.

The Job of the Executor or Trustee

The executor or trustee must see that tasks of settling an estate are executed, however they do not have to be the one physically completing the tasks. They are the project manager.

The executor or trustee must <u>keep track of all time and expenses incurred during administration</u> *to facilitate compensation from the estate for eligible services and expenses.* Keep receipts for all expenses for purposes of accounting to the heirs and possible estate tax return deductions (See Chapter 2, Federal Estate Tax.) Consult an accountant.

The executor or trustee should contact the organizations listed in the previous section, *contacting Social Security immediately* and the others as soon as possible.

They must also <u>prepare a list of the deceased person's assets</u>. As soon as the executor or trustee has a list of creditors, they should notify the credit reporting agencies. This is important to minimize the risk of identity theft. Contact all three national credit reporting agencies by telephone:

Experian   888-397-3742
              P.O. Box 9701 Allen, TX 75013
Equifax   800-685-1111
              P.O. Box 740256 Atlanta, GA 30374
TransUnion   800-888-4213
              P.O. Box 2000 Chester, PA 19022

Request that the credit report be flagged "Deceased. Do Not Issue Credit."

Follow up with a written request sent via certified mail. <u>The written request should be formatted as follows:</u>
"Notification of Death"
Request for "Deceased, Do Not Issue Credit" Notation

For Decedent Account -
Name of Decedent:
Most recent address:
Date of Birth:
Date of Death:
Social Security Number:
Because it is being mailed, I would put only the last four digits followed by "Please contact for full number."

Requesting Party Information:
Your name:
Your street address:
Your relationship to the decedent
Your phone number:

Relationship to Decedent & My Proof of Authority
I am decedent's surviving spouse: include a copy of their marriage certificate
I am a court-appointed representative of the estate: include letters testamentary or trust document

Request for Credit Report
Please send a copy of decedent's current credit report to me at the above address. See proof of authority above.

Sign and date the above and send to the credit reporting agencies by certified mail.

Contacting the Professionals
As soon as possible, the executor or trustee needs to:

Contact the Lawyer
- If the person settling the estate is an executor (as opposed to a trustee who has immediate authority), <u>the executor must petition the probate court for recognition as the executor and acquire a letters testamentary to be used as proof of legal authority</u>
- If the person settling the estate is an executor, ask what documents must be filed with the courts in regard to the estate (assets, receipts, etc.)
- Ask what time constraints you are under for specific tasks such as paying creditors, filing taxes, etc.
- Discuss whether the assets are sufficient to pay the debts and whether any allowances are provided for the surviving spouse.

Contact the Accountant

- Get an employer identification number for the estate from the IRS, if necessary.
- Arrange for the preparation of income tax returns and file final individual income tax returns and any fiduciary and estate tax returns which are necessary. Follow the normal schedule of tax due dates.
- File a federal estate tax return within nine months after death if required, although most estates are not large enough to owe federal estate tax.
  👀 👀 👀 Verify whether the first spouse to pass must file a federal estate tax return, even if no federal estate tax is owed, in order for the portability option of the estate tax exclusion to apply to the surviving spouse.
- File a state estate tax return, usually within nine months after death if required, although fewer than half the states impose their own tax.

Contact the Financial Advisor/Planner

- Discuss the value of having an estate account.
- Discuss any investments that need to be transferred to a beneficiary and determine how that will happen.
- If any qualified retirement account such as an IRA is inherited, discuss any *Required Minimum Distributions* **that may be required.**
- Discuss any inherited trusts and any requirements to withdraw the annual trust income to avoid taxes. Any amount of trust income not distributed, usually over a designated amount, may be subject to tax at the highest bracket.
- Discuss the fact that the tax basis of certain assets must be adjusted to the date-of-death value.

After Contacting the Professionals

- Consider keeping at least one bank account with the decedent's name on it open for depositing any outstanding checks (refunds, insurance settlements, etc.).
- Keep credit cards open <u>until after all possible refunds have been credited</u>. Then close them.
- Notify all banks and investments with a death certificate and a copy of either the letters testamentary for rights as the executor or the living trust for rights as the trustee.
- Keep an accounting of all estate income and expenses.
- Collect any sources of income including paychecks, Social Security, Veterans benefits, pensions, insurance policies, investments, refunds such as premiums paid, etc. Sources will have to be notified of the decedent's death so appropriate payments may begin or end.

  🐞🐞🐞 <u>Social Security will require payback of funds already paid for the month</u>. The monthly payment to Social Security for medical coverage (usually deducted from the monthly payment to the recipient) is not refundable. The executor or trustee must reserve the amount to be returned to Social Security until it is collected by Social Security.

- Contact decedent's employer (and possible former employers) for information on pension, 401(k), life and medical insurance, death benefits, accrued vacation pay and any other benefits.
- Contact all <u>creditors</u>, pay debts (state law may impose a deadline on you) and close accounts. The court may require that you file a list of creditors' claims you have approved and denied.

- Cancel medical, life, and long- term care insurance.
  🐞🐞🐞 <u>Do not cancel home or auto insurance</u> until the distribution/disposition of the property has been completed and a new policy has been obtained.
  Make a claim for proceeds on any insurance policies that pay out, such as life insurance.
- Appraisals for all material assets such as real estate, business interests, automobiles and jewelry will be required. If you have questions about whether an appraisal is required, contact your lawyer.

Distributing the Assets of an Estate

Once the immediate things have been addressed, and all income and liabilities have been resolved, the executor or trustee has the authority to disburse the assets to the beneficiaries according to, and in the following order:

1. terms of a living trust and
2. terms of the last will and testament

🐞🐞 Asset distribution identified through tenancy and beneficiary designations (including POD and TOD) are accessible only by the beneficiary. If the beneficiary is a trust, then the asset will fall under the terms of the trust.

You will need to:

- Notify the heirs and beneficiaries that the final distribution is coming up.
  🐞🐞 Beneficiary distributions are last, after creditors.
- Transfer assets to the new owners and get receipts. This may require the signing of legal documents. Some assets may have to be retitled. A letters testamentary or death certificate may be required. Consult your lawyer and

financial advisor in regard to the required process for transfer and any necessary documents.

Strategy for Sorting Through the Personal Property of an Estate

You may now be faced with the often overwhelming task of sorting, distributing and disposing of the personal property of an estate. If you view this as a project that requires managing and develop a plan with a strategy that includes subprojects, the task will become doable.

👀👀 When a Google search is suggested below, be sure to add your town/city name either at the beginning or end of the search criteria to find results in your area.

👀👀 Keep in mind that if you are working in a home for long periods of time, you may need dishes, cleaning supplies, garbage bags and paper goods such as toilet paper and paper towels.

The executor usually has complete authority

It is the executor's responsibility to see that those assets of the estate that are not in a living trust are distributed according to the will. They do not physically have to do all the work, but they are responsible for seeing that the work is done according to the terms of the will. The executor can ask family members or an estate settling company for assistance.

Most often the assets not in trust are the contents of a home. Many times the directions of a will specify that the executor is to split the assets equally among siblings. The sorting and distributing of assets can be a nasty interaction among siblings. In the end, the executor usually has complete authority to determine the distributions, as long as they are equitable.

111

The following identifies a process my sisters and I used to sort through our parents' estate. Our parents' home contained their belongings and some belongings of three of our grandparents. While the sorting and distributing of parents' assets can be a bone of contention for many siblings, our method allowed for equality and peace. Much of this method still applies for an individual sorting and distributing.

Schedule a meeting to create a game plan
My sister, the executor, scheduled a meeting with our other sister and me, the three who would be involved in helping to sort and distribute the personal property. The executor must be present every time property is handled. And the executor is the one to schedule future work dates, coordinating with all those involved. The executor is the project manager of the process.

During our first meeting, we agreed to treat the process like a business project requiring a commitment, schedule, plan and strategy. This approach allowed for some of the emotion to dissipate. While of course it was an emotional process to go through our parents' belongings, we were largely able to work through subprojects with a business perspective.

We discussed our goals and priorities for the project. We had several goals:
1. To put the home on the market for sale by a specific date
2. To place or sell vehicles by a specific date
3. To find a home for as many items as possible, and to donate or recycle everything else, with the goal of creating as little trash as possible

We developed a strategy for daily work sessions. Each day we would identify exactly on which subproject we would focus.

At the end of every workday, we would remove what had been processed. We would stop work about ½-1 hour before the end time to log all donations that had been identified, tidy up and load our cars. We would dispose of all trash, drop off donations, and take items home that we had been given. We agreed to start bringing boxes and bags to use for moving items. We would also need a couple of notebooks for documenting distribution decisions and itemized donations.

As I said, we were particularly concerned with seeing that as many items as possible would be used by someone. For items that our family and friends could not use, we had the following options.

- Sell

  My experience with selling items was that it is not very productive. Garage sales have been virtually replaced by craigslist and eBay. When we did use craigslist or eBay, we listed items as "must pick up," cash only and price not negotiable. When the customer arrived to pick up the item, we met them outside the house and always with someone else present. When we listed an item as "FREE", we placed bets on how many minutes it would take for someone to call on the item. We received a call on a FREE king size mattress in 8 minutes and it was picked up in under 15 minutes. While estate sales are beneficial for quickly disposing of items, they often result in very low income. Discuss this with any service you may consider.

- Donate

  Our criteria for donations was that the item was in good shape and could be used again. If clothing was ripped and or badly stained, it became either a rag or trash. Other items had to be in working condition. We

113

considered to which organization each item would be donated. Our parents felt strongly about some charities (homeless veterans, women's, literary, sewing, quilting and fishing organizations), and we tried to donate to them whenever appropriate, even when it would have been easier to donate someplace else. We considered the demographic for donation as well and donated to senior community and living centers. Finally, all other donations were taken to organizations such as Goodwill or picked up by AMVETS.

🐞🐞 Itemized donations can be divided among siblings. Contact an accountant about how to properly report those donations.

- <u>Recycle</u>
  There are many types of recycling.
  - o <u>Paper, plastics and glass</u> were put in residential recycling. Although my parents' community had recycling bins, we often took the recycling to our homes in order not to burden their community.
  - o <u>Household hazard</u> (paint, oil, cleaning products) <u>and electronics</u> usually require disposal during a community drop-off event. Call your town, or check your town's website, to inquire as to any upcoming dates.
  - o <u>Books and magazines</u> can be donated to libraries and senior living and community centers. You may also be able to take books to resale bookstores. Rare books should be appraised.
  - o <u>Medications</u> may need to be disposed of because they have expired or because they are no longer needed. Expired medications can be disposed of in various ways depending on the community. Some allow drop off at specific locations such as a fire station or

grocery store and others offer community drop off events. If the medications have not expired, they are not narcotics and you can see the medication name, dosage and expiration date on the label, it can be donated to a local veterinary clinic for use on animals.

o Eyeglasses can be dropped off at Walmart optical departments. Some locations have a drop off box for the Lion's Club. Both organizations will make use of the donation.

o Hearing aids – Google "hearing aid recycling" and call local audiologists.

o Dentures can be taken to their dentist to arrange to have any gold removed and paid for.

o Pacemakers – contact the supplier to return it for use of the data. Try Googling "recycle pacemaker." Some states allow the pacemakers to be reused but there are strict specifications.

- Shred
Any confidential documents, or those containing private information, that are no longer needed should be shredded. There are companies that do onsite shredding for a very reasonable price. They typically want a minimum amount, such as filling a 96-gallon bin. Google "onsite shredding" followed by your town name. School supply stores usually offer shredding services and are good for small quantities. Some communities offer shredding services, in conjunction with their electronics and household hazard collection events, for a nominal fee or donation. Many churches offer free shredding services. Some service businesses, such financial planners, offer complimentary shredding to their clients.

- Trash

  Out of respect for the community in which our parents had lived, we often brought trash home with us. If we had a small quantity and the community bins were empty, we might put some in it. Again, one of our goals was to create as little trash as possible. For large items we called a trash company to prearrange pick up. Junk removal/hauling companies will haul almost anything for a nominal fee.

Shortly before we started to go through our parents' home, I began reading the book *The Life Changing Magic of Tidying Up*, by Marie Kondo. As I read, I realized that we had automatically begun to follow many of the things that she proposes, such as categorizing like items and identifying subcategories. The most valuable recommendation, and one that we found invaluable, is identified further below.

We decided to address <u>those tasks that seemed the least emotional</u>, and therefore easiest, in the following order:
1. Creation of staging zones: boxes and bags for use, trash, recycling, donations, papers to be shredded, etc.
2. Collection and disposal of actual trash
3. Collection and separation of mail, magazines, catalogs and important papers such as bank statements, insurance claims and letters
4. Creation of a couple of "special" boxes: one for papers and another for items such as cards, letters and photos that we were not emotionally ready to process at the time and wanted to keep for sorting and processing at a later time

We then decided to <u>work room to room</u>.

Our first step was to take items that belonged in other rooms to those rooms for processing at a later time. Next we categorized and organized items, taking any items belonging in a predefined zone to that zone. For example, if we had already set up a zone for books, we took all books to that zone. We would identify projects within the room and work on them one by one.

We started in our parents' bedroom. Our first step was to go through their closet, much of which we knew we would be donating. We had previously donated most of our dad's clothing, but a few sentimental items of dad's clothing were left in addition to our mom's clothing. We did the following with the clothing and every other category we had to process.

- Identified subcategories
- Processed one subcategory at time, such as pants, tops, purses and shoes
- Determined whether any of the three of us wanted or could use the item
- If not, we would identify if any of the grandchildren might want or use it
- If not, we would identify if any of our close friends or caregivers might want or use it
- If not, we would evaluate if the item was in good enough condition for donation
- If so, we then decided which type of donation business was best suited for the item
- If not, we determined if the item could be recycled and how
- If not, it was considered trash

It usually took us a matter of seconds to run through the determination process for each item. With clothing in particular, we took the time to evaluate which organization would most benefit from an item. For example, we took the majority of Dad's clothing to a home for male veterans that works to get men employed and independent within six months. Some of Dad's dress clothes could be used for interviewing. We took Mom's dress clothes to a shelter that works to employ the homeless and place them in their own apartment within 120 days. Again her clothes could be helpful in interviewing. The extra effort it took to drive to various locations, based on the items we were donating, was worth it to us.

We methodically worked our way through the bedroom and repeated the process for items in drawers such as underwear and sweaters.

Once the work in the master bedroom was completed I requested that we do <u>a walkthrough of the home looking only at furniture and large items</u>. I was overwhelmed by the fear that we were going to have to dispose of much of the furniture and other large items, and it was really stressful for me. I asked that we create a list of those items, and that we each indicate if we were interested in taking it, not interested or unable to take it, or if a grandchild might be interested. It was not a commitment, but rather a barometer that gave us an idea of the amount of furniture, particularly large items, for which we might need to find homes. It eased my stress to realize that in fact, we really could place most of the furniture within our family. Of course, the actual items might have changed by the end of the process, but it was a good first indicator. An added benefit of that process was that my perspective began to change. Before, I thought that I already had all the furniture I needed for my home, but I began to realize that I had the opportunity to upscale some items.

Also, in discussing the disposition of furniture, we realized that because we would be selling a home, we might need to defer the actual removal of some of the furniture. It required that we envision staging the home and identifying what furniture we wanted in place during showings. We then knew which pieces would have to wait to be removed from the property, whether by a person or for donation, until after the sale of the property.

As we returned to the room-by-room approach we identified more subcategories, of items found throughout the home that needed zones such as:

- Coats, hats, gloves, boots
- Bathroom items such as first aid, personal care, nail care, dental, etc.
- Cleaning supplies
- Household items such as a vacuum, an ironing board
- Linens: towels, sheets, pillows
- Collections
- Books
- Gift wrap
- Kitchen items such as: storage containers, spices, baking goods, glassware, dishes, appliances
- Silver, crystal, china, specialty items
- Jewelry
- and any other item of which there were multiple

Subcategories not only organized items but also defined for us a contained project to do when we simply could not face something larger.

As we moved from practical items and encountered more sentimental items, we needed a way to process them. Kondo recommends holding each item and asking:

- Do I have use for it?
- If I take it, do I have a place to store it?
- Does it bring me … joy? If the answer is yes, ask further if the joy was in the past or if it currently brings joy?

Kondo also elaborates to explain that many times, especially with sentimental items, we feel obligated to take them. But then, after we do, they are stored and unused. She offers the idea that, while sometimes the joy is in using the item, other times it comes from the purchase and the item never even gets used. Sometimes the joy is in the memory, especially with clothing, and the item just sits in the closet. If the joy is not current, then let the item move on to a person for whom it will bring joy. That idea was invaluable to my sisters and me during this process. When we encountered an item that had brought us joy, usually in a memory, but whose usefulness for us had passed, we would all put our hand on the item and take a selfie of the three of us with it. We could then let the item move on to its next place of joy.

For all items, if one of the three of us gave the item to a parent, the giver could take the item outright. It did not count as an item they selected.

We had a process for dividing subcategorized items: For example, decorative items were further separated into like items, such as vases and figurines, and placed together. Of course, the "whoever gave it, gets it" rule applied to these items. Afterward, we had a strategy for item selection:

1. We asked if any sister was interested in a particular item in a category/subcategory. If so, and there was no

objection from another sister, then the other sisters could either agree on which items they wanted or draw numbers for order of selection.

2. When no one had a particular interest, all sisters drew a number and selected an item of their choice in their selected number order. After one round of selections, numbers were redrawn again for the next selection.

3. Within a category, if there were not enough items for everyone to make another selection, the items could be held for selection with other unclaimed items at a later time, or it could be mutually decided that a non-sister (grandchild, caregiver, friend, another relative) be given an item.

4. After the sisters had selected from a category, and we had tried to place items with other relatives, we considered close friends and then opened selection up to our caregivers

Finally, we had one category each for our parents that were a bit unusual and required some thought, research and effort in disposal. Our mom had been a seamstress and had also created an international in-home quilted pillow kit business. She therefore had a lot of sewing supplies and fabric which were donated to those who would most appropriately use it. Our dad had been a fisherman from the age of 4 and had not only fished streams and big lakes but was also a charter boat captain. To say that he had a lot of fishing equipment would be an understatement. We were able to sell small boat fishing equipment but had no market for large lake fishing supplies. Therefore, we contacted a fishing organization in Chicago, of which Dad was a founder, and shipped everything to them to be sold as part of their annual fundraising. Was it easy,

NO. Was it the right thing to do, yes. And while we did not receive payment for the items, we were able to claim a tax deduction, as the organization is a tax exempt not-for-profit. Both our mom and dad would be happy with our decisions on donating their special possessions.

A note about selling our parents' home. Instead of waiting until we had processed everything in their home, we decided to list their home at the point when we had moved out all furniture and large items not being kept for staging. We still had closets filled with things to be sorted and cabinets containing dishes and serving pieces to be divided, all of which could be taken out, worked on and restored prior to another showing. We figured that we had several months before we would sell the home and have to be completely out of it. The surprise for us was that we sold their home for over asking price, cash, no contingency and before the home actually appeared on the market. Therefore, we had to work nonstop for several weeks. Each of us took home several boxes marked "special," and we rented a storage unit for another month. While not optimal for us, it did allow us to be out of the home in time for closing.

After selling our parents' home and emptying the rented storage unit, my sisters and I took a desperately needed break from processing the items in the estate. Over time we continue to go back and process the "special" boxes, containing photos and emotionally charged items such as jewelry, as we have the time and inclination. Allowing for the passing of some time greatly reduces the emotional charge connected with the items, making it significantly easier to make good decisions about dividing them.

Closing an Estate

After all assets have been distributed and all estate matters are concluded, the executor must initiate the process to legally close the estate and probate. The type of probate process by which you have been working will determine the process necessary for closing and releasing you from your duties. Most processes require some sort of reporting on the content and distribution of assets, as well as any compensation paid for services and expenses of the executor. Contact a lawyer for direction on the process necessary for your situation.

Sometimes the hardest part
isn't letting go,
but rather learning to start over.
Nicole Stevens

Chapter 8

MOVING FORWARD ...

a new normal

I wish that I could tell you that it gets better. More so than "better," it becomes "different." Things will never be the same, but that doesn't mean that it can't be good again.

> You never stop loving someone,
> you just learn to live without them.
> Unknown

Finding your new normal requires finding a new balance, understanding that finding balance includes being off balance, incorporating your life prior to loss with that loss. There are healthy ways in which to incorporate your loss through memorializing the life that has passed. For me, I incorporated family heirlooms and items of personal value into my home. I created a memory book of the end-of-life process, condolences and the family celebration of my parents' lives. On each of my parents' birthdays I celebrate differently, by doing an activity that they enjoyed or making a champagne toast to them. My husband's family uses video chatting to connect and make a martini toast to their mother. On the anniversaries of their deaths, we also do something to celebrate their memory.

> There will come a time
> when you believe everything is finished.
> That will be the beginning.
> Louis L'Amour

🐞🐞🐞 A note on guilt. Sometimes as time passes, guilt can arise that causes you to question whether or not you did the right things and did enough. In Chapter 1, Crisis Management, Information, Friend or Foe, I stated my philosophy on decision making. As long as I adhered to it, I had no reason for guilt. If you made the best decisions you could with the information you had at the time, and you did the best that you could in your circumstances, the answer to whether you did the right things and did enough is yes. The guilt is unreasonable. If guilty feelings persist, it may help to discuss them with a therapist, whether or not they are unreasonable.

Thoughts on Grief

For me, somehow knowing what to expect was helpful. It allowed me to let go of criticizing myself, feeling as though I was out of the norm, feeling alone in the process.

Grieving the loss of a loved one is very different than fixating on the actual moment of loss. That moment was only one during the lifetime of the person. To fixate on it dishonors all of the other moments of their life. You can grieve your loss and celebrate their life at the same time.

Grief is a process. Sometimes it begins at diagnosis and sometimes it begins at the time of a person's passing away. At either time, it can affect you not only emotionally but also physically and mentally. It can cause fatigue, depression, mental fog and forgetfulness, inability to focus, appetite changes and digestive issues, insomnia, headache, aches and pains, shortness of breath, anxiety and more frequent illness. While it is important to acknowledge that these symptoms may be caused by grief, if any of them escalate or continue, seek professional diagnosis and assistance.

There is no one way of grieving and no set length of time that it lasts. The process is individual. For me, at first it was intense and seemingly endless. When my dad passed away I remembered Queen Elizabeth II's words in regard to the death of Princess Diana. She said, "Grief is the price we pay for love." Shortly after he passed away, I received a note from a dear childhood friend. It concluded with, "He died knowing that you loved him and you live knowing that he loved you. That is beautiful and the love will last forever." Both were a great comfort to me.

Your grief is your love, turned inside-out.
That is why it is so deep.
That is why it is so consuming.
When your sadness seems bottomless,
it is because your love knows no bounds.
Unknown

As time passed, my grief began to ebb and flow and came at the most unexpected times. I could be perfectly fine, not thinking about someone who had passed and whom I missed, and then something in a store would trigger a memory and I would find that I was instantly crying.

Ever had a memory that sneaks out of your eye,
and rolls down your cheek?
Unknown

Throughout my grieving processes, I have come across several things that resonated with me and helped me to understand what and how I was feeling, as well as to move through the grieving process.

A few months after Dad's passing, I came across a story on Facebook, from the perspective of an elderly man, that accurately described the grieving process I was experiencing.

An excerpt:
I wish I could say you get used to people dying. But I never did. I don't want to. It tears a hole through me whenever somebody I love dies, no matter the circumstances. But I don't want it to "not matter". I don't want it to be something that just passes. My scars are a testament to the love and the relationship that I had for and with that person. And if the scar is deep, so was the love. So be it.

Scars are a testament to life. Scars are a testament that I can love deeply and live deeply and be cut, or even gouged, and that I can heal and continue to live and continue to love. And the scar tissue is stronger than the original flesh ever was. Scars are a testament to life. Scars are only ugly to people who can't see.

As for grief, you'll find it comes in waves. When the ship is first wrecked, you're drowning, with wreckage all around you. Everything floating around you reminds you of the beauty and the magnificence of the ship that was, and is no more. And all you can do is float. You find some piece of the wreckage and you hang on for a while. Maybe it's some physical thing. Maybe it's a happy memory or a photograph. Maybe it's a person who is also floating. For a while, all you can do is float. Stay alive.

In the beginning, the waves are 100 feet tall and crash over you without mercy. They come 10 seconds apart and don't even give you time to catch your breath. All you can do is hang on and float. After a while, maybe weeks, maybe months, you'll find the waves are still 100 feet tall, but they come further apart. When they come, they still crash all over you and wipe you out. But in between, you can breathe, you can function. You never know what's going to trigger the grief. It might be a song, a picture, a street intersection, the smell of a cup of coffee. It can be just about anything...and the wave comes crashing. But in between waves, there is life.

Somewhere down the line, and it's different for everybody, you find that the waves are only 80 feet tall. Or 50 feet tall. And while they still come, they come further apart. You can see them coming. An anniversary, a birthday, or Christmas, or landing at O'Hare. You can see it coming, for the most part, and prepare yourself. And when it washes over you, you know that somehow you will, again, come out the other side. Soaking wet, sputtering, still hanging on to some tiny piece of the wreckage, but you'll come out.

Take it from an old guy. The waves never stop coming, and somehow you don't really want them to. But you learn that you'll survive them. And other waves will come. And you'll survive them too.

If you're lucky, you'll have lots of scars from lots of loves. And lots of shipwrecks.

Author Unknown

Around the first anniversary of my dad's passing, only 3½ months after my mom passed, I felt as though something was not quite right. A friend explained to me that while I was experiencing the first anniversary of my dad's passing, I was in deep grief over my mom's passing. She explained that I still had to reach the first anniversary of my mom's passing, and to move on to the second anniversary of my dad's passing before I would begin to feel whole again. She helped me understand that I felt as though a piece of me had gone with both my dad and mom when they passed, and said that around the second anniversary I would begin to feel that I had assimilated them back into me. She could not have been more accurate in her description and the timing.

> In French, you don't say
> "I miss you."
> You say "tu me manques,"
> which means,
> "you are missing from me."
> I love that...
> Unknown

Grief is not something that can be rushed, nor should it be. You don't have to "get over it," stop talking about it, or move on ... right now.

> Within each of us there is a cemetery of sorrow. It is a legitimate place where the losses throughout our lives accumulate, and one we must visit repeatedly to do our grief work. Grief is often untidy. We can't wrap our losses in fine stationery and tie it up with a bow. Instead, they come layered in memories, regrets and unresolved conflicts. So to revisit our cemetery is healthy, because grief is often ongoing and done in seasons. Visits are necessary for our well-being, as long as we don't' take up residency among the tomb. And while we must grieve (…) we might re-enter life more able to offer grace.
> Patsy Clairmont from *Twirl...A Fresh Spin at Life*

Following are a few more perspectives on why we should not hide our grief nor hide from it.

> If instead of pretending we are okay, we would take the time to wail, to weep, to scream, to wander the woods day after day holding hands with our sadness, loving it into remission so it doesn't turn cold inside of us, gripping us intermittently in the icy fingers of depression. That's not what grief is meant to do.
> Alison Nappi, Excerpt from 5 Lies You Were Told About Grief

> And herein lies the gift that cannot die. It changes the course of your life forever. If you allow yourself the chance to feel it for as long as you need to — even if it is for the rest of your life — you will be guided by it. You will become someone it would have been impossible for you to be, and in this way your loved one lives on, in you.
> Alison Nappi, Excerpt from 5 Lies You Were Told About Grief

> Grief is a matter of the heart and soul. Grieve your loss, allow it in, and spend time with it. Suffering is the optional part. Love never dies, and spirit knows no loss. Keep in mind that a broken heart is an open heart.
> Louise Hay & David Kessler

If you find yourself taking up residency at the cemetery of sorrow, seek help. Your grief is real and sometimes it takes others to help us take the first steps toward our new normal. Letting go of grief is not the same as letting go of your loved one. It is healthy to leave behind the pain and sorrow and to carry beyond it only the memories and experiences that enhance your ability to find peace.

The work of Elisabeth Kubler-Ross is an excellent resource on grief.

Then when it seems we will never smile again,
life comes back.
Mark M. Baldwin

Your Losses Are Not Your Identity

For many the process of loss is greater than grieving and finding a new normal. It can involve pain, guilt, unanswered questions and a variety of emotions that can prevent you from moving forward. Some find themselves stuck in a repetitive cycle of hopelessness and unable to allow themselves to experience joy and pleasure. For others, the loss can begin to define or consume them, causing a loss of identity.

Many years ago I watched an episode of the Oprah show on which there was a mom whose daughter had a tragic death. She was imprisoned by her grief, having lost her way out. I think that she may have felt that to stop grieving would mean that she was letting go of her daughter. In a single moment, Oprah pointed out to the mom that she was choosing to focus on only the one moment of death, instead of celebrating all of the valuable moments of life. She was stuck in her grief and she needed to move forward.

Moving forward is easier said than done. There are many paths to moving forward, most of which include seeking the help of any of a variety of professionals. Professional therapy is just one path.

Another path is to learn through the experience of others who have lost loved ones. In Deb Sheppard's book *Grieving to Believing, Discovering the Afterlife*, she writes about the process of finding a path beyond grief to a life again filled with joy. When Sheppard faced what was an overwhelming heartbreak, she discovered that there was a light ... *the light* ... waiting for her at the end of her tunnel. As I said previously, energy cannot be destroyed and is rather transitioned into another form upon death. Sheppard is able to access the energy of loved ones who have passed. *Grieving to Believing* will show you how to have the very best life you can under any type of circumstance.

Personally, having adhered to a strict 24x7 care schedule through my parents' care and transitions, I then found myself lost. Literally overnight, the responsibility and constraints required for 2 ½ years were lifted, and I didn't know how to construct my day. I had no idea what to do with my new free time. I was exhausted and it took the better part of a year for me to regain my physical and mental strength. During that time, I heard the calling to write books based on my experience and to create a platform to help others on the care path. But, I was tired, a bone-deep tired, and I did not know what the next phase of life held for me. While it was tempting to sit back and enjoy retirement with my husband, I also felt that it would be a shame to discard all of the information I had amassed while caregiving. I was conflicted.

In February of 2017, I attended Soulful Living I, a workshop presented by a dear friend and her co-founder, aimed at helping attendees to define their life purpose and to navigate the next phase of life. It sounded perfect. Honestly, I attended so that I could finally silence the voice that kept telling me to write books and help others. I failed at my mission. After completing the workshop, I realized that I had to follow my calling. I took the first steps forward and started writing what has become the Comfort in Their Journey book series. The Soulstice Group (www.SoulsticeGroup.com) provides workshops, including the Soulful Living series and Daring Way, which is based on the work of Dr. Brene Brown, to support people in building resilience and recovery, defining their purpose and meaning, and discovering how to live in a more wholehearted and authentic way. I highly recommend their work.

> The first step towards getting somewhere
> is to decide that you are not
> going to stay where you are.
> J. P. Morgan

Moving forward may take time, it may take several attempts to find what works for you and it may require the assistance of a professional. Whatever your path, take the first step forward and don't stop.

If you live to be 100,
I hope that I live to be 100 minus 1 day,
so I never have to live without you.
Winnie the Pooh

Chapter 9

FINAL THOUGHTS ...

and additional reading

As stated in the Preface, my expertise is derived from the full-time care of my parents, one with Alzheimer's, for whom I delivered the care and end-of-life that they desired. In addition, I had the privilege of assisting my mother-in-law with her transition. Peaceful Endings provides the practical guidance I wish had been readily available to me and was not. I had to develop the steps that allowed me to be present during the entire process and able to have the following awareness during and perspective immediately after their transitions.

My dad, in his home surrounded by his family, peacefully passed away with dignity. That day I shared:

> Today my dad transitioned into pure light and love. It is said that grief is the price we pay for love - amen. My great-nephew captured my sentiment when he said, "Grampy is always sad when you leave because he loves you so much." I know the feeling. I love you Dad ... always and forever.

The following day I shared:

> 92 years of life.... 69 years of marriage (72 years of friendship with my mom) and over 26,000+ "I love you"s (if only one was said per day, and most days it was many more). I feel like I said that many in the last 21 months. I am blessed to have had my dad (and to still have my mom) for so many years, yet how could it have gone so fast? STOP, L O V E - truly love - those who are

important to you, no matter what is going on in your life. Love your parents NOW, as they are gone too soon, no matter how many years you have them.

It has been an honor and a privilege to care for my dad for the past 21 months (and to continue to do so for my mom), and to ensure that he pass on his own terms. I have learned more from them in that time than I have in all my combined years prior. Dad is my hero, the kind who saw the best in everyone and said that if he could do it, they could too.

I wrote the following a little over eight months later:
For the second time in eight months, it is with overwhelming sadness that I say that someone I love, my mom, peacefully transitioned into pure light and love. A 2 ½ year journey came to an end today resulting in a light that is now both my mom and dad. My heart is completely full of gratitude for every second that I spent with my parents. The void that is left is truly unfillable, as I have already known the two best people that I will ever know.

I am more tired than I knew a person could be, as the things that I have had to face during these years have been more difficult than those faced in the collective 55 years prior. I am grateful that my husband, family, my old and cherished friends, my new and invaluable friends and my parents' caregivers (who have become not only friends but extended family for life) understand and know that one day I will again be strong. In the meantime, I am grateful for the little face of Maggie May (my puppy) who looks at me with her soulful eyes each morning as if to say, "Come on, it's a new day, get up and play with me" and I know everything will be ok.

Mom, I need your grace to find my own. I made you and Dad a promise 2 ½ years ago, and I did my very best for you and Dad. It has been an honor and a privilege to have you as my parents, to care for you both, and to see that you both left this life from your home and on your own terms. I love you both .... always and forever!

Eighteen months after the passing of my mom, my mother-in-law was diagnosed with terminal cancer. She passed away six weeks later. While caring for my mother-in-law, I sat down and wrote about my experience. This is an excerpt from that writing, which I read as a eulogy:

In the past several weeks I have had the privilege and true honor of being a part of the family caregiving team providing care for Dottie. It is quite an experience to accompany someone you love down the final path of their life. As each family member went through the tunnel of shock, realization, anger, and then resigned acceptance, Dottie was the steadfast beacon of light showing the way. All worldly events became unimportant and dropped away from our family as our lives began to focus entirely on Dottie and her needs, of course with concern for Carl and each other. Our family came together in a 10x12 room, where all of life focused on providing Dottie with comfort. And for Dottie, all the responsibilities that for years had defined her daily life no longer existed. What was left was a woman surrounded by the love of our family and her friends, and asking only for one possession: her rosary. When all earthly things fall away, and the body has served its purpose as vessel to the soul, what shines through is the true essence of the spirit, and Dottie's was crystal clear blue, pure, and full of all that really matters: faith and love.

What a gift she gave us all. Her amazing spirit set the tone for our entire family, even through her last breath. The strength and grace with which she lived is not only admirable but now sets the bar to which each of us can reach.

Through Dottie's last breath she lived a meaningful life and I, for one, have been forever changed by knowing her. It's true that grief is the price we pay for love. But her love is also what will bring us through the grief. My husband says his mom "peacefully went to sleep and stayed in her dreams." I would add that she thereby transformed our memories into starlight, which will go on forever.

Do not stand at my grave and weep,
I am not there, I do not sleep.
I am the ladybug that stops to say hello,
I am the diamond glints on snow.

I am the butterfly that flitters by,
I am the patchwork of colors in the evening sky.
The gentle summer rain guarantees,
I am the wild flowers swaying in the breeze.

Of quiet birds in circled flight,
I am the moonlight on the lake at night.
Do not stand at my grave and cry;
I am not there,
I did not die.
By Mary Elizabeth Frye, adapted by Nancy

While this book is specific to dealing with crisis and the process of end of life and beyond, there is additional information that is needed if the journey involves providing care such as: creating a care plan and caregiving. Following is a list of some of the topics covered in *Through the Rabbit Hole* and *A Most Meaningful Life* that serve as a supplement to the information in *Peaceful Endings* and guide the way through dignified caregiving.

Through the Rabbit Hole details the following and more:
- Crisis management
- A new responsibility
- Care options and approaches
- Worthwhile assistive items and durable equipment
- Dealing with specific medical issues

There are several sections of *A Most Meaningful Life* that, although specific to Alzheimer's and expanded upon in *Through the Rabbit Hole*, are relevant to everyone and presented from a different perspective.
- My Family's Philosophy
- The Ultimate Goal
- My Family's Strategy

Afterglow
I'd like the memory of me
to be a happy one
I'd like to leave an afterglow
of smiles when life is done.
I'd like to leave an echo
whispering softly down the ways,
of happy times
and laughing times,
and bright and sunny days.
I'd like the tears of those who grieve
to dry before the sun,
of happy memories that I leave
when my life is done.
Helen Lowrie Marshall

When I am gone, release me. let me go. I have so many things to see and do. You mustn't tie yourself to me with tears. Be happy that we had so many years.

I gave you my love, and you can only guess how much you gave to me in happiness. I thank you for the love you each have shown. But now it's time I traveled alone.

So grieve a while for me, if grieve you must. Then let your grief be comforted by trust. It's only for a while that we must part. So bless those memories in your heart.

I won't be far away for life goes on; So if you need me, call and I will come. Though you can't see me or touch me, I'll be near. And if you listen with your heart, you'll hear all my love around you – soft and clear.

Unknown

Approximately 55 percent
of American adults do not
have a will or other estate plan in place.
LexisNexis

AFTERWORD ...

pre-emptive preparedness or
the best gift you can give to those you love

No one wants to talk about end-of-life planning, but understanding and creating the plans and documents necessary for the end of life is possibly the best gift you can give to those you love. Estate planning takes time, involves costs, asks hard questions and requires organization of necessary documents. On top of that, it uses a different language (see Chapter 2.) But, completing and documenting your estate plan removes the stress of your loved ones having to guess what you would want. It also makes settling your estate a much easier process. In addition to estate planning, financial planning is critical. Whether you are a current caregiver or will require care in the future, a clear financial plan allows those involved in care to understand the financial boundaries and resultant care options.

In answering the question of when to create your estate and financial planning, the answer is that if you have not already done so, do it **now**.

I recommend that everyone start their estate planning at age 18, the legal age of adulthood in the United States. As a legal adult, they must make all medical decisions for themselves and their medical information is private and no longer accessible by parents. When my daughter turned 18, I asked her if she wanted the E.R. doctor who had never met her to make life and death decisions for her or if she preferred one of her parents, who love her, to make those decisions for her. In addition, 18 is the age at which people begin to move away from home and often request assistance from their parents to obtain medical records, which is no longer possible due to their age and the Health Insurance Portability and Accountability Act. This was true of my daughter. Due to both of the scenarios described above, she decided to assign medical power of attorney to me, which she can terminate at any time she chooses.

An 18-year-old should create a will and:
1. Power of attorney
2. Durable power of attorney for health care
3. Declaration as to medical or surgical treatment
4. Burial/cremation instructions
5. Gift under Uniform Anatomical Gift Act (organ donation, if desired)
6. Tangible property list
7. Letters to the executor and beneficiaries stating wishes

As discussed in Chapter 2, an advance directive specifies what actions should be taken for a person's medical care if they are no longer able to make decisions themselves.

This can be specified in a living will or by using a Five Wishes document, a form of living will in lay persons' terms that also helps express personal and spiritual desires pertaining to end of life care. Five Wishes documents can be used in all 50 states and meet legal requirements in 42 states and D.C. Visit https://www.agingwithdignity.org/ to learn more and to download the document.

After preparing the above documents, estate-planning documents should be reviewed and possibly updated with each important life event: marriage, divorce, birth of children, acquisition of assets, retirement, etc.

Again, as the best gift you can give your loved ones, it is better to have something in place that can be easily updated as life changes, rather than having nothing legally documented.

What to Have Prepared

In preparing and organizing your estate information, you should create a set of files. The lists in this section will guide you. A cover page is provided for each file, on which you will checkmark any Section/Folder in which you have documents. Then for each Section/Folder page, checkmark the specific items for which you have documents. In addition, <u>always note if there are "Other" items, not individually listed, included in the Section/Folder</u>.

Once you have done so, **notify your power of attorney and executor so they know where to look in the event of your incapacitation or death.**

SUMMARY of FILES

☐ **SECTION/FOLDER I:** *General Information*

☐ **SECTION/FOLDER II:** *Legal documents and Heirs/Beneficiaries*

☐ **SECTION/FOLDER III:** *Assets and Liabilities*

☐ **SECTION/FOLDER IV:** *Employment/Retirement*

☐ **SECTION/FOLDER V:** *Insurance*

☐ **SECTION/FOLDER VI:** *Property*

☐ **SECTION/FOLDER VII:** *Financial Plan and Investments*

☐ **SECTION/FOLDER VIII:** *Personal Belongings*

☐ **SECTION/FOLDER IX:** *Taxes*

☐ **SECTION/FOLDER X:** *Other Estates and Fiduciary Capacities*

☐ **SECTION/FOLDER XI:** *Internet User Ids/Passwords*

SECTION/FOLDER I: *General Information*

Information Needed for a Death Certificate:

- ☐ Full legal name of deceased, maiden name, gender, date of birth, place of birth

- ☐ Father's name, mother's name and their places of birth and birth dates

- ☐ Address, including county

- ☐ Social Security number

- ☐ Marital status, spouse's full name

- ☐ Level of education

- ☐ Occupation

- ☐ Military Service, branch, years

- ☐ Date and time of death, age, place of death

- ☐ Manner of death (natural, accident), cause of death

- ☐ Method of disposition (burial/cremation), place of disposition

- ☐ Informant of death and relationship to deceased

List of People to Notify:
full name, relationship and contact info

☐ Family

☐ Friends

☐ Professionals/providers including: clergy, executor, attorney, accountant, financial advisor, insurance agent, VA, Social Security, Medicare, Medicaid, bank, physicians, dentist, hair stylist/nail tech, other providers

☐ Business associates (employer, employees, clients, retirement plan):

Name and Contact Information for:

☐ Lawyer

☐ Financial advisor/planner

☐ Accountant

Safe Deposit Box:

☐ Location, number and names of signers

☐ Inventory of contents

SECTION/FOLDER II: *Legal Documents and Heirs/Beneficiaries*

<u>Original</u> Legal Documents in Regard to Estate Planning, Medical/Surgical Treatment and Final Wishes

- ☐ Last will and testament

- ☐ All trust agreements and amendments
    - o Living and any other trusts for the benefit of the individual

- ☐ Power of attorney

- ☐ Durable power of attorney for health care

- ☐ Declaration as to medical or surgical treatment

- ☐ Burial/cremation Instructions: see Chapters 4 and 5 for information needed

- ☐ Gift under Uniform Anatomical Gift Act (if desired): www.organdonor.gov or a copy of your participation as indicated on your driver's license

- ☐ DNR (if desired)

- ☐ Advance directive

List of All Known Family Members and Beneficiaries

- ☐ Full name, date of birth, relationship, address and phone number

SECTION/FOLDER III: *Assets and Liabilities*

Cash and Promissory Notes

- ☐ Name, contact info, web user id/password and approximate balance of all bank accounts

- ☐ All bank records - checking, savings, trustee and POD accounts

- ☐ Bank statements for the past twelve months (may require web user id/password)

- ☐ Checks payable to decedent uncashed at date of death

- ☐ Amount and location of cash not in banks

- ☐ Promissory notes payable to Decedent

Miscellaneous Assets

- ☐ Business interests, including corporate or LLC records and partnership documents

- ☐ Accounts receivable, including debtors and amounts

- ☐ Social Security death benefits.

- ☐ Uncashed Social Security checks

- ☐ Unpaid Medicare and health insurance reimbursements

- ☐ Club and lodge memberships

- ☐ Veterans benefits

Liabilities

- ☐ See *"List of all bills"* below

- ☐ Current monthly Social Security payment, <u>which may have to be returned to Social Security</u>

- ☐ Outstanding checks written by or on behalf of Decedent

- ☐ Balance on credit card statements

- ☐ Unpaid debts, including names and addresses of creditors, amount and reason

- ☐ Secured and unsecured promissory notes and guarantees signed by Decedent

- ☐ Security agreements on personal property for debts owed by decedent

- ☐ Funeral bills, including cemetery, flowers, plot, memorial services, luncheon, etc.

List of all bills: *Name, contact info, approximate balance*

Home
☐ Mortgage/rent
☐ Association dues
☐ Property taxes
☐ Security system
☐ Lawn care

Phone (landline, cell)

Utilities
☐ TV
☐ Internet
☐ Electric
☐ Gas
☐ Water/sewer
☐ Garbage/recycling

Credit cards

Insurance
☐ Home
☐ Personal Property, including riders (jewelry, art, furs, etc.)
☐ Cars/vehicle
☐ Umbrella
☐ Life
☐ Medical
☐ Drug
☐ Dental
☐ Vision
☐ Long-term care
☐ Other (dues, etc.)

SECTION/FOLDER IV: *Employment/Retirement*

Employment/Retirement Benefits

- ☐ Unpaid salary, commissions, or bonuses

- ☐ Employee benefits

- ☐ IRA, 401(k), 403(b), ESOP and Profit Sharing statements

- ☐ Accrued unemployment and insurance benefits

- ☐ Pension benefits

- ☐ Union benefits

SECTION/FOLDER V: *Insurance*

Insurance Policies, all kinds, Agent Contact Info

- ☐ Home

- ☐ Personal Property, including riders (jewelry, art, furs, etc.)

- ☐ Cars/vehicle

- ☐ Umbrella

- ☐ Life (on decedent, on others for which decedent paid premium)

- ☐ Medical

- ☐ Drug

- ☐ Dental

- ☐ Vision

- ☐ Long-term care

- ☐ Other (dues, etc.)

SECTION/FOLDER VI: *Property*

Titled Property

Real Estate

☐ Deeds and title policies

☐ Promissory notes/mortgages

☐ Current and preceding years' tax bills

☐ Insurance policies and agent contact information

☐ Leases

☐ Contracts

☐ Land Trust documents

☐ Trust agreements and/or partnership agreements

☐ Encumbrances and liens of any kind

Motor Vehicles: Title, Registration, License and Loan amounts.

☐ Cars

☐ Other vehicles: boats, motorcycles, RVs

Joint Tenancy Assets

☐ All papers, deeds, bank accounts, etc., of every kind on which decedent's name appears as a joint tenant (possibly residence.)

☐ Name and address of each joint tenant.

SECTION/FOLDER VII: *Financial Plan and Investments*

Financial Planning:

- ☐ Current financial plan

- ☐ Investments

- ☐ Brokerage account statements.

- ☐ Stock certificates and book entry or dividend reinvestment plan statements

- ☐ Mutual fund statements

- ☐ Bonds, including United States savings bonds.

SECTION/FOLDER VIII: *Personal Belongings*

Personal Belongings: *inventory, description*, estimated value

- ☐ Collections

- ☐ Jewelry

- ☐ Furs

- ☐ Artwork

- ☐ Heirlooms

- ☐ Antiques

SECTION/FOLDER IX: *Taxes*

Tax Returns

☐ Name and address of decedent's accountant

☐ Personal and business, both federal and state, income tax returns for last three years

☐ Tax payments or refund information

☐ State and federal gift tax returns filed by decedent

SECTION/FOLDER X: *Other estates and fiduciary capacities*

Estates in which the individual has or had an interest

Fiduciary capacities of individual – Trustee, Executor, Administrator, Guardian, Conservator, etc.

SECTION/FOLDER XI: *Internet:*

User ids/Passwords
List account type (email, credit card, creditor), website, user id, password
Note: this list may be online or in the cloud

Accounts to be Deleted

In addition:
Include several spiral notebooks for taking notes for medical episodes, estate settlement, etc.

What You Need to Do to Create a Will

To create a will, you can either do it yourself with the use of an online template from various websites or use other information and directions found on the internet, or you can seek the services of a lawyer.

My recommendation is to make the necessary decisions, and then contact a lawyer to draw up the legal documents, as laws vary by state and non-compliance may result in the will being invalid. Thinking through your decisions before meeting with a lawyer will greatly reduce the time required of the lawyer and therefore the cost.

In **some states**, a holographic will may be an option. A holographic will is a last will and testament that has been handwritten and signed by the creator, eliminating the need to work with a lawyer and to have a witness or notary present for signing. They are often chosen for their ease of creation, ease of superseding (overriding) a previous will, and are sometimes the only choice in emergency situations when a lawyer is not available.

- It must be <u>handwritten and signed</u>.
- Witnesses and a notary are **not** required but, when possible, may be beneficial.
- It identifies that this is your new will and supersedes any previous wills.
- Lists name, children's names, executor, and asset distribution.
- The **original** should be given to someone trusted. The **original** must be available upon death.

🐞🐞 A holographic will is a good choice for someone who is unable to work with a lawyer. It is also a good choice for young adults with few assets.

If you choose not to work with a lawyer, sign and initial each page of your will. Do not make any changes to the will after it has been signed. Check what your state requires for signatures and witnesses.

In any will, burial wishes can be included, however they are not enforceable. The executor can decide not to follow the wishes (for example, if they can't afford it), but any family member can contest it in probate court. Judges typically side with the decedent's wishes.

Your executor will be identified in your will. While you are creating a will, consider creating these additional documents usually associated with the will.
1. Power of attorney
2. Durable power of attorney for health care
3. Declaration as to medical or surgical treatment
4. Burial/cremation instructions
5. Gift under Uniform Anatomical Gift Act (organ donation, if desired)
6. Tangible property list
7. Letters to the executor and beneficiaries stating wishes

🐞🐞🐞 It is best to create a list of people to assume the roles of power of attorneys, executors and guardians. There are several things to know about assignment of responsibility.
1. Responsibility is given to those identified in the order listed. If the first person listed is deceased or is unable or unwilling to accept the responsibility *and relinquishes it,*

the responsibility passes on to the successor listed next in numerical order.

2. You must decide if you want only one person to have the responsibility or if you want multiple to concurrently share the responsibility. This is particularly helpful when 1. a parent wants a young adult child who lives nearby to have power of attorney but also wants them paired with an older adult who may not be nearby or 2. there are multiple siblings who may share in the responsibility.

3. Often spouses list each other as their power of attorney and executor. It is always important to identify successors.

4. For power of attorneys, you must specify if their authority is activated upon your incapacitation or immediately active while you retain your right to terminate their authority.

5. It is beneficial to have your list of guardians match that of your spouse.

Finally, many community and senior centers offer workshops on estate planning document preparation, including notarization, for a reasonable fee. You may want to contact a lawyer to review your decisions.

For your Will:

1. Your full legal name, Social Security number and address

2. You must declare that:
   - This is your Last Will and Testament.
   - You are of legal age and sound mind.
   - Your wishes do not result from undue influence.
   - This document nullifies all previous wills.

3. Identify family members: spouse, children, grandchildren.

4. Identify and empower your executor *and successors*.

5. Identify the assets you can bequeath.

6. State the division of your assets.

7. Specify the distribution of particular assets, including any conditional gifts. (See Chapter, Last Will and Testament.)

8. Specify provisions for predeceased beneficiaries. Decide if the asset is returned to the "pot" to be split equally among the other beneficiaries per capita or if the asset is to pass on, per stirpes, to the deceased beneficiary's descendants. (See Chapter, Last Will and Testament.) Also specify the desired distribution of all assets in the event that no designated beneficiaries survive you. This is known as a "disaster clause" or "ultimate distribution," and often identifies a charitable organization.

9. Designate a list of guardians *and successors* to minor children in the event that you are deceased.

10. State special requests such as what is to happen with your remains.

The Value of Comprehensive Financial Planning

Financial planning, working with a financial planner or advisor, allows you to make the right choices for your future goals and to ensure your well-being, including care toward the end of life.

Regardless of whether the title is financial planner or advisor, these professionals should provide both planning services, which include everything from budgeting and tax advice to estate planning, and investment management. When looking for a financial professional, you want to find one who interviews their clients to understand their short-term and long-term goals and objectives. Professionals with a CFP®, Certified Financial Planner certificate, are recognized as holding the standard of excellence for competent and ethical personal financial planning. Selecting a professional who can provide _unbiased guidance without the influence of a product to sell_ is invaluable.

The planning and advice can provide clarity in several areas including:
- Identifying and setting goals, including events, travel, retirement and end of life.
- Creating a budget based on income and expenses.
- Establishing an emergency fund.
- Planning for savings, investing and debt payoff.
- Reviewing insurance needs including auto, home, health, life (especially if there is family to protect) and long-term care insurance (See *Through the Rabbit Hole*).
- Creating a strategy for increasing income.
- Understanding tax matters.
- Creating tax-efficient strategies for estate planning.

After a plan has been created, it is important not only to follow your plan but also to continue to work with your professional when changes arise and to review your plan on a regular basis.

A clear financial plan is a critical piece to estate planning which will facilitate the process if, in the future, someone must assume responsibility for your finances and/or care.

I'm a strong person
but every once in a while,
I would like someone to take my hand
and tell me
that everything's going to be all right.
Unknown

POSTSCRIPT ...

how to help someone in crisis

The first thing to understand is that a person in crisis needs help. They may not be able to ask for it. Sometimes they are too exhausted to know what they need or to even make the effort to ask for help. Everyone in a tough situation can use support. There is helpful support and misguided support. Knowing the difference makes all the difference to the one in need.

Move Love Inward, Throw The "Trash" Outward
Often at the height of a crisis, people find that they not only feel they don't know what is appropriate or helpful to say but that they in fact have said the wrong thing unintentionally.

For decades I have been aware of my relationships with others, even distinguishing between real friends and acquaintances, where real friends are let into an imaginary circle allowing them to be closer to me than acquaintances who reside in a circle further away from me. _Susan Silk, a clinical psychologist, and Barry Goldman describe a way to use that imagery to help identify what is and is not appropriate and helpful for others to say to someone in a crisis situation._ They suggest the following, which I have enhanced.

Draw a circle and write the name of the person in crisis in the center.

Draw six more circles, each larger and outside of the previous.

Label the circles, starting with the circle closest to the original, as follows

circle #2:   immediate family: significant other, children
circle #3:   close family: parents, siblings
circle #4:   true friends
circle #5:   colleagues
circle #6:   acquaintances, distant relatives
circle #7:   anyone else

The rule is simple: send your *love inward* and your *"trash" outward*.

The person in the center can say anything, positive or negative, to anyone at any time.

For every other circle, the intention is to help those closer to the crisis, those in the smaller circles. Therefore, listening is more helpful than talking, which should provide only comfort and support. Advice should not be given to those in a smaller circle, only love and support get put in. "Trash", complaining or unhelpful personal experience or information, should be shared with bigger circles only. The trash should always be dumped out.

Most people know not to dump trash into the center ring, but many don't realize that it is never helpful to dump into any smaller circle.

Susan Silk is a clinical psychologist. Barry Goldman is an arbitrator and mediator and the author of "The Science of Settlement: Ideas for Negotiators."
OpEd piece in the LA Times 2007
http://articles.latimes.com/2013/apr/07/opinion/la-oe-0407-silk-ring-theory-20130407

What You Can Do to Help Someone in Crisis

The needs of people are variable during a time of crisis. The intensity of the crisis will ebb and flow, and with it the needs. Some crises are a sprint to a cure or a premature end and others a marathon of treatment and care. Every situation is different depending on whether the person is at home or in a facility, there are caregivers and which type, how long the crisis is likely to last and what will happen once the crisis is resolved. The person in crisis may be the caregiver (spouse, family member, friend) and/or the person needing care.

Some people will be able to provide emotional support, others logistical support and others will be organizers. If everyone uses their strengths to provide help, the person in crisis will be lifted up as much as possible.

First, ask…. "How can I help?" If you get an answer, do it. If you do not get an answer, make a suggestion, such as asking if receiving a dinner would be helpful. Sometimes people are not comfortable with accepting help, let alone asking for it. It is optimal if the person can articulate their needs. If not, sometimes it is easier for them to acknowledge whether or not a specific offer would be helpful at that time, and the offer allows them to suggest something different such as lunch instead of dinner. If you hear hesitance in their voice, you can always drop something off at their home and make it clear that you do not expect to stay and visit. If they are in need of a visit, they will invite you.

Gift cards to restaurants, in particular those offering carry out, are thoughtful. Sometimes having a gift card is the difference between whether or not the person stops to get food.

If the crisis is ongoing, you can offer to set up a calendar of food/meal deliveries, errands to be run, housecleaning etc. Ask for a list of people to contact.

Respite for the caregiver comes in many forms. If appropriate, something to brighten the person's day is nice. Think in terms of something they particularly enjoy: flowers, a sweet treat, a message, a book, or anything that will provide a moment's respite from the stress. Respite might include a visit with the person in crisis, allowing an intellectual and emotional respite for the caregiver, as well as the person being cared for, by changing the focus for a brief time. If the situation requires full-time care, a longer visit can provide the caregiver time to recharge and rejuvenate.

Whatever the method, support from friends is often what keeps someone dealing with a crisis afloat. Something as simple as a message saying that you are thinking about them can make all the difference in their day. And never underestimate the power of just listening or lending a shoulder on which to cry.

OTHER RESOURCES

Listed are few of the resources that I found most helpful. Visit www.TrishLaub.com for more resources.

The Comfort in Their Journey Book Series by Trish Laub
A Most Meaningful Life
      my dad and Alzheimer's
Peaceful Endings
      guiding the walk to the end of life and beyond
Through the Rabbit Hole
      navigating the maze of providing care

Alzheimer's

Alzheimer's Association
www.Alz.org
The Alzheimer's Association is an invaluable resource for anyone affected by Alzheimer's. Provides family consultation and support groups, classes, a 24-hour bilingual helpline, and safety programs that are available free of charge through individual state chapters.

Be with me Today
      A challenge to the Alzheimer's outside
By Richard Taylor, Ph.D.
DVD: HaveAGoodLife.com
A psychologist and professor diagnosed with Alzheimer's at 58 explains what it is like to have the disease, how people treat him and how they should treat him – that there is a person in there.

Contented Dementia
By Oliver James
Based on the SPECAL (Specialized Early Care for Alzheimer's) method, this book delves into the feelings and past memories that remain intact in a person living with Alzheimer's, and how both can be used to create links to the loss of more recent information.

Gates Notes, the blog of Bill Gates   www.gatesnotes.com
Why I'm digging deep into Alzheimer's blogpost

I'm Still Here
    A New Philosophy of Alzheimer's Care
By John Zeisel, Ph.D.
I'm Still Here is a guidebook to Dr. Zeisel's treatment ideas, showing the possibility and benefits of connecting with an Alzheimer's patient through their abilities that don't diminish with time, thereby offering a quality of life with connection to others.

The Spectrum of Hope,
    An Optimistic and New Approach to Alzheimer's
    Disease and Other Dementias
By Gayatri Devi, M.D.
The author defines Alzheimer's as a spectrum disease that affects different people differently. She encourages early treatment which enables doctors and caregivers to effectively manage the disease, allowing those diagnosed with it to continue to live fulfilling lives.

Dignified Care

Being Mortal
Medicine and What Matters in the End
By Atul Gawande
In the inevitable condition of aging and death, the goals of medicine too frequently run counter to the interest of the human spirit. This book offers examples of freer, more socially fulfilling models for assisting the aging and end of life.

Honest Medicine
Shattering the myths about aging and health care
By Donald J Dr. Murphy, M.D.
Dr. Murphy sets the record straight on popular myths, mistakes and misconceptions in regard to the controversial issues associated with health care for older patients and the importance of understanding the pros and cons of treatments.

Learning from Hannah
Secrets for a Life Worth Living
By William H. Thomas, M.D.
Through storytelling, this book addresses the value of elders to the community as a whole and focuses on 10 principles necessary to meet their needs which include eliminating the three greatest causes of suffering: loneliness, helplessness and boredom. The 10 principles have become the basis for a real-world project, the Eden Alternative, dedicated to creating quality of life for elders and their care partners, wherever they may live.

Life After the Diagnosis
　　　Expert Advice on Living Well with Serious Illness
　　　for Patients and Caregivers
By Steven Z. Pantilat, MD
A guide to living well with serious illness and getting the best
possible end-of-life care.

End of Life

The Life Changing Magic of Tidying Up
    The Japanese art of decluttering and organizing
By Marie Kondo
This book offers a strategy for sorting through volumes of items, identifying what to keep and what to pass along.

When Breath Becomes Air
By Paul Kalanithi
A neurosurgeon's perspective as a patient with stage 4 lung cancer and the question of what makes a life worth living.

When Souls Take Flight
    coping with grief
By Kira Rosner
A non-sectarian view of what happens when we die, with compassionate advice for anyone who is grieving.

180

ABOUT THE AUTHOR

In 2002 Trish Laub was told that her father was being treated for Alzheimer's. Originally from Chicago, she and her husband moved to the Denver area in 2012 not only to enjoy the beautiful mountains but also to be closer to her parents.

Just 48 hours after Trish arrived in town, her father experienced an unexpected medical crisis, setting into motion a two and one-half year journey of care. Trish served as not only a caregiver but also as manager of both the care team and her parents' medical care. The process continued through their end of life and the settlement of their estate, and has since included the care of her mother-in-law and consulting for others. In all, over a period of five years, Trish has gained over 12,000 hours of experience in providing care for a loved one, including one living with Alzheimer's, taking the final walk of their life with them, and settling their estates.

After spending 18 years developing computer systems, Trish went on to co-found both a national dance education company and a national nonprofit prevention theater company focused on helping at-risk teens. She is a Black Belt instructor of The Nia Technique and has been licensed since 1999. Using her previous computer and teaching experience in combination with her most recent caregiving experience, Trish has created Comfort in Their Journey to provide practical guidance for dignified care through end of life.

Trish Laub

Author | Consultant | Speaker

AUTHOR

Trish is available to present her book series to your audience and to offer signed copies.

SPEAKER

Schedule Trish to bring her expertise to your group. Trish offers a variety of presentations on Alzheimer's, crisis management, end-of-life and dignified care, or can create a custom presentation for your group. She presents concise and specific information that is immediately useful, and inspires her audiences with the goal of teaching others to provide compassionate and dignified care.

CONSULTANT

Consult Trish for guidance on meeting your caregiving needs. Trish is available to help you address your caregiving needs by discussing care options and answering your questions.

www.TrishLaub.com
720-288-0772

THE COMFORT IN THEIR JOURNEY
BOOK SERIES

A Most Meaningful Life
my dad and Alzheimer's
a guide to living with dementia

A Most Meaningful Life
my dad and Alzheimer's

a guide to living with dementia

Trish Laub

A Most Meaningful Life tells the story of a daughter's journey through Alzheimer's disease with her father, from her initial awareness of his diagnosis to navigating his care and helping him achieve the good death that we all deserve. It is the story of how Alzheimer's affected her father's life and the lives of those who loved him, as well as the story of her family's successes and failures throughout the journey. With her family's efforts, creativity and desire to preserve their father's quality of life for over a decade, he continued to truly live a meaningful life through his final days.

Through the story of her journey, the author offers a new perspective, the determination that even with Alzheimer's, the possibilities are limitless. With a clear philosophy and the creation of a strategy, others can have a roadmap to navigate their loved one's journey so that they have "A Most Meaningful Life."

Peaceful Endings
guiding the walk to the end of life and beyond
steps to take before and after

Peaceful Endings
guiding the walk to the end of life and beyond

steps to take before and after
Trish Laub

The topic "no one wants to talk about," end of life and beyond, is exactly what *Peaceful Endings* addresses. Many times the end of life is preceded by illness and caregiving, and may also include a variety of crises, as life changes and decisions must be made quickly. Whether proactively preparing for the end of life, or facing it imminently, there are medical, legal, financial, insurance and care decisions to be made, each with its own specific language. The author walks the reader through the terminology, the choices and the process of the end of life. The author also details what must be done after the transition, and provides perspective on stepping into a new normal after a loved one's life has ended.

Through the Rabbit Hole
navigating the maze of providing care
a quick guide to care options and decisions

Through the Rabbit Hole

navigating the maze of providing care

a quick guide to care options and decisions

Trish Laub

Through the Rabbit Hole is exactly the reference book that the author needed for quick access to information during her experience providing care for her ill parents. It wasn't available for her, so she has written it for all the families and caregivers who are now beginning their journeys. Her parents' medical crises caused her to fall down the rabbit hole and into the maze of unfamiliar options and decisions. Having emerged from the maze, the author details the complexities of caregivers and facilities, the need for patient advocacy, as well as the medical, legal, financial and insurance aspects of care. With the end goal of compassionate and dignified care, this book, a wonderful companion to *A Most Meaningful Life*, is a beacon through the maze of care.

Comfort in their Journey
with Trish Laub

Whether during an illness or injury, or at the end of life, I hope that you have found your purchase helpful in your journey of providing compassionate and dignified care.

VISIT THE COMFORT IN THEIR JOURNEY WEBSITE

Go to www.TrishLaub.com to check out everything Trish has to offer including a blog containing new information and topics not covered in the book series.

While you are there… please send us a review to post.

COMING IN SPRING 2019

The CitJClub membership including access to the information in all three books in the series, including search capabilities across all three books, and much more.

Your purchase of this book qualifies you for a discounted CitJClub membership.
Visit www.TrishLaub.com for more information.
720-288-0772